Betty & Nancy
With much love
from
Constantia -

MARY ELEANOR BOWES, COUNTESS OF STRATHMORE

THE UNHAPPY COUNTESS

and her Grandson John Bowes

RALPH ARNOLD

CONSTABLE · LONDON

By the same author

Novels
HOUSE WITH THE MAGNOLIAS
HANDS ACROSS THE WATER
SPRING LIST

Topography and History
THE HUNDRED OF HOO
A YEOMAN OF KENT

First published in Great Britain 1957
by Constable and Company Limited
10 Orange Street, London WC2H 7EG
Paperback edition 1987
Printed in Great Britain by
St Edmundsbury Press Limited
Bury St Edmunds, Suffolk

ISBN 0 09 468180 5

Contents

Illustrations

Acknowledgments

I COULD not have written the biographical sketches of Mary Eleanor, Countess of Strathmore, and of her second husband, if Jesse Foot, Surgeon, had not published his *Lives of Andrew Robinson Bowes, Esq., and the Countess of Strathmore, written from thirty-three years' Professional Attendance, from Letters, and other Well-Authenticated Documents*; and if Bowes had not printed and published his wife's *Confessions*.

The accuracy of the *Confessions* is discussed in the course of the narrative. Foot's biography is trustworthy so long as he relies on his personal association with Bowes and on the letters mentioned in the sub-title of his book. It is when he draws on 'the well-authenticated documents' that his narrative goes astray, as in his account of Lady Strathmore's abduction, which he lifted bodily from the *Gentleman's Magazine*.

Foot, called in for the first time when Bowes was wounded in his *rencontre* with Parson Bate, seems at first to have been fascinated by his patient and flattered by his patronage. He was quickly disillusioned, but that did not prevent him from frequently dining and occasionally staying with Bowes; and he continued to visit him until the end of Bowes' life. He never met Lady Strathmore before 1777, and thereafter saw her only occasionally.

In the introductory chapter to his *Lives* Foot adopts a tone of high moral indignation: 'It will be seen that all the adventitious appendages and decorative ornaments of fortune have not corrected their nature, enlarged their felicity, fortified their virtue, nor shielded their lives from the miseries consequent to vicious habits, unbounded passions, and lawless perpetrations. . . . Neither of them received one single

9

Acknowledgments

check from any compunctious visitings of nature; neither of them had disciplined their minds by the strict observance of any rule of right; both of them appeared as if they had been taken from a land not yet in a state of civilization, and dropped by accident where they have been found.'

This wholesale condemnation, which illustrates Foot's love of long words, is almost certainly unfair to Lady Strathmore's memory. Much of Foot's information about her came to him at second hand and from hostile sources. There may not be a great deal to be said in her favour, but there is more than Foot allows.

I could not have written the biographical sketch of John Bowes without the generous help of Mr. Thomas Wake, F.S.A., Curator of the Bowes Museum and Park, and without access to the papers, books, letters and newspaper cuttings preserved in the Museum and made available to me by kind permission of the Museum's Trustees. But neither Mr. Wake nor the Trustees must be held responsible for any expressions of opinion found in this book.

I am indebted to the Hon. David Bowes Lyon for the loan of original material and for allowing me to reproduce the portrait of Mary Eleanor, Countess of Strathmore, which hangs at St. Paul's Walden Bury. The Earl of Strathmore has permitted me to reproduce portraits of George Bowes and of the 9th and 10th Earls, which are at Glamis. Francis Askham's *The Gay Delavals* (Cape) provided invaluable information about that family. Among others who gave me generous help were: Mrs. Joan St. George Saunders, Mr. Charles Ogden, A.R.I.B.A., Col. E. H. Kirkup, Baron Henry de Gelsey, Mrs. Robert Graham of Fintry, Mr. R. L. Edwards, Q.C., Mr. Joseph Dean, Mr. Christopher Hussey, Miss Dorothy Stroud, Mr. Tom Ingram, Mr. Michael Harrison, Mr. James J. F. Kemp, and the City Librarian, Newcastle upon Tyne.

Author's Foreword

'NEVER trust a man with a hyphen' was a piece of advice which is said to have been given by Edwardian mothers to their marriageable daughters. But there are some 'compound' surnames which are so firmly established by long usage that they can hardly be thought of save in their familiar conjunction—and high in this category is the patronymic Bowes Lyon, the family name of the Earls of Strathmore and Kinghorne.

This book tells how and why the 9th Earl of Strathmore and his eldest son, the 10th Earl, substituted the surname of Bowes for that of Lyon; and why, whereas the 11th and subsequent Earls coupled the two surnames together, the only son of the 10th Earl was styled Mr. John Bowes.

The story behind these changes in nomenclature spans three distinct periods of English social history—the second half of the eighteenth century, the Regency, and the Victorian era; and it must be left to the reader to judge whether the three people principally involved—Mary Eleanor, Countess of Strathmore, her son John, 10th Earl of Strathmore, and her grandson, John Bowes—can be said in any way to have reflected the characteristics of the periods in which they lived.

These three very different people, whose lives overlapped three very different epochs, had something in common besides their blood relationship. They shared a common and well-defined background.

'Background' was another word employed by Edwardian mothers when confronted with prospective sons-in-law. 'Yes,' they demanded anxiously, 'but what is his background?'

By 'background' they meant a number of different but

related things which appeared to them to be of considerable importance. They meant: what kind of a family does he come from? Is there a family 'place'? Is there money and, if so, what is its source?

These questions were probably asked for all the wrong reasons; but, basically, there was some sense in them, for the young man might reasonably be expected to inherit, to a greater or lesser degree, the established traditions of his family; the ownership of land and of a great house might well influence both his tastes and his career; while the extent of inherited wealth, and the source from which it was derived, could hardly fail to be reflected in his outlook, conduct and opportunities.

The main line of the family of Bowes of County Durham and Yorkshire ended in 1767 with the marriage of an only child and heiress, Mary Eleanor Bowes, to John Lyon, 9th Earl of Strathmore. Thenceforward, for two generations —for the lifetimes of Mary Eleanor, Lady Strathmore and of her eldest son, the 10th Earl—it was the Bowes traditions, the Bowes properties, and the Bowes wealth which, for better or for worse, played a determining part in the destinies of the Strathmore family. It was not until the Committee of Privileges of the House of Lords had dismissed John Bowes' petition to succeed his father as the 11th Earl that the Lyons returned to Glamis Castle and to their earlier traditions, leaving Mary Eleanor's grandson in sole possession of the Bowes inheritance.

All these events are now distant enough in time to be safely disinterred and examined for what they were—a very strange interlude in the long history of a great and distinguished family.

CHAPTER ONE

All the Wealth of the North

THE Bowes family of Streatlam Castle, in the County Palatine of Durham, traced their ancestry back to Sir Adam Bowes, a successful fourteenth-century lawyer who had obtained Streatlam near Barnard Castle by his marriage to the Trayne heiress; and thereafter successive eldest sons, the most notable of whom was Sir George Bowes, Queen Elizabeth's powerful supporter at the time of the Rising of the North, married into most of the great north country dynasties. In 1691, by marrying the only child of the last Blakiston baronet, Sir William Bowes, Mary Eleanor's grandfather, added Gibside, near Gateshead, to the already extensive family properties.

The ownership of a large acreage of agricultural land in County Durham and in Yorkshire was very well; but it was not from the rents and fines from the small grazing farms of the day that real wealth derived. To survive and flourish, County Durham landowners had to take advantage of their hidden riches; and it was the Blakistons,who had blazed that trail. The last two Blakiston baronets of Gibside had successfully exploited their ownership of coal-bearing land near the south bank of the River Tyne, and Sir William Bowes had gone a step further by helping Ambrose Crowley to establish his iron works at Blaydon. William Blakiston Bowes, Sir William's eldest son, was equally astute, opening new pits further from the river and deriving considerable revenue from constructing the first ancestors of the railways—the wooden-railed wagon-ways which connected the inland pits with the staiths or landing stages on the river bank.

The Unhappy Countess

In 1722 George Bowes, Mary Eleanor's father, most unexpectedly succeeded to the family properties, his two elder brothers having died unmarried within a space of twelve months. He was twenty-one years old and, as good or evil fortune had it, he proved to be a most forceful and successful man of affairs.

The coal trade in County Durham was a curious business. It was the responsibility of the coal owner to get his coals from his pit to his staith on the Tyne. At the staith, his 'fitter', a hostman (or guildsman) of Newcastle upon Tyne, exercised his historic right of taking the coal over and of transporting it in flat-bottomed keels to one of the colliers anchored in the river mouth. The ship's master, having purchased his cargo outright from the 'fitter', carried it to the Port of London where he sold it to the London Lightermen, who in their turn passed it on to the members of the Woodmongers' Company, monopolist coal merchants in virtue of their former connection with the sale of charcoal. This long retail chain produced endless difficulties, and throughout the eighteenth century Durham coal owners struggled hard, but in the main fruitlessly, to exercise some effective control at the various points where the coal changed hands. To meet the pretensions of the Newcastle hostmen, the monopolies enjoyed by the ships' master, the Lightermen and the Woodmongers, and the protests of successive Lord Mayors of London against any rise in retail prices, the principal Durham coal owners, George Bowes among them, formed a coal trade partnership, known as the Grand Allies; and it was largely to further the aims of this partnership that George Bowes, having spent £5,000 in unsuccessfully contesting the Borough of Berwick in 1725, succeeded two years later in getting himself returned as one of the two members for the county. He continued to represent Durham in the Whig interest until his death in 1760.

He made only one recorded speech in the House, but he was an unwearying lobbyist, fighting on grounds of his own choosing which often brought him into collision with his coal trade partners. It had been the custom of the Durham coal

owners to pay premiums—in other words bribes—to the
London Lightermen in order to ensure the rapid unloading
of Newcastle coal cargoes. After the Grand Allies had agreed
to discontinue these payments, George Bowes disbursed as
much as £3,000 in a single year. When his partners decided
to re-start the payments, George Bowes elected to pay
nothing. He embarked on a one-man policy of price cutting,
to the despair of his partners but to his own very considerable
profit. In the end it was generally George Bowes' policy that
prevailed. He was a man who knew what he wanted and
who generally got it. What he wanted was great wealth and
the best of everything.

When he left school, where he had idled, there had been
talk of his being apprenticed to a London merchant, but the
thousand-pound premium had dismayed his close-fisted
mother who, instead, had bought him a commission in the
army; and when he succeeded to the family estates he was a
captain in a cavalry regiment. As a very young man he had
been exceptionally handsome and very wild. In 1724, his
prospects having dramatically changed, he married Eleanor
Verney, only child of the Hon. Thomas Verney. Eleanor
Verney was fourteen when he married her, and already a
prodigy of learning—'the most accomplished of her sex'
as he sadly noted when she died in the following year. He
remained a childless widower for twenty-two years, and then
he married Mary, heiress of Edward Gilbert, of St. Paul's
Walden in Hertfordshire. Mary Eleanor, born on February 24th, 1749, was his only child, his heir, and the apple
of his eye.

George Bowes was one of the most popular men of his
time and it is easy to see why, for he had charm and a great
zest for living; and he combined a love of all field sports
with an appreciation of beauty both in nature and in
art.

He introduced fox-hunting into County Durham. In 1738
he bought nineteen couple of hounds and three terriers from
Sir William Middleton of Belsay Castle in Northumberland;
and in 1745, 'at an immense price', he acquired a celebrated

pack of fox hounds belonging to Thomas Fownes, of Steeple-
ton Iwerne in Dorset—'the first pack of English hounds to
be entered solely to fox'. His father, Sir William Bowes, had
owned and raced thoroughbred horses which he had bred at
Streatlam Castle—among them the celebrated Byerly Turk
mare. George Bowes enlarged the Streatlam stud, and in
1753, with Cato, won the first race for the King's Purse run
on the Town Moor at Newcastle upon Tyne. Among other
famous horses he bred were Whitefoot, Miss Hewet, Lady-
legs, Othello, Snake and Miss Dixon.

When he succeeded, Gibside was not the principal family
seat, for his eldest brother, William Blakiston Bowes, had
nearly completed the rebuilding of Streatlam Castle, the
original Bowes stronghold. George Bowes may have disliked
Streatlam's low-lying situation or he may have preferred his
own romantic taste to his brother's severe classicism; at all
events it was at Gibside and not at Streatlam Castle that he
made his home, it was on Gibside that he expended half a
lifetime of affectionate care, and it was at Gibside that he
undertook one of the most notable landscape layouts of the
century.

To the house itself, built by William Blakiston between
1603 and 1620 on a ledge above the River Derwent, George
Bowes did little beyond adding a projecting north wing in
the same Jacobean style. But he had begun planting the
steep ravines of the river bank in 1729, and in 1747 he started
work on the mile-long terrace which runs east and west in
front of the house. In 1750, with James Paine as his architect,
he embarked on a building programme which included a
banqueting house in the Gothic taste, a classical stable block,
a bathing house, an immensely tall stone column surmounted
by the figure of Liberty, and an orangery. Work on the
mausoleum-chapel, which was to crown and complete his design, was begun in his lifetime, and in his will he left his
executors £8,000 with which to finish the undertaking after
his death. Each of these buildings was carefully designed and
placed in a scheme of landscaping which depended for its
effect on an approach by way of the serpentine drive which

GEORGE BOWES, M.P.

GIBSIDE

runs along the face of the river bank to the open plateau
or ledge on which the house stands.

Even today, when the hanging beech woods have been
long felled, when all the buildings save the chapel and the
column are crumbling ruins, and when the drive itself is
little more than a mossy track, the approach to the roofless
shell of Gibside is still a rewarding adventure in skilfully
delayed anticipation.

That George Bowes was an artist with a real talent for
landscaping is proved by the fact that he did not call in one
of the established landscape gardeners of the day. There is
no evidence whatever for the statement, often made, that
Capability Brown worked at Gibside. George Bowes did the
job himself, employing Paine to design his buildings. Indeed,
the Column of British Liberty, save for its crowning figure,
which was carved by Christopher Richardson on the spot, was
erected at the cost of £2,000 exclusively by estate labour.

He showed the same good taste in his purchase of pictures,
furniture and objets d'art for his house. He paid fifteen
hundred guineas for Rubens' painting of the artist's wife,
enceinte, in a fruit shop; he commissioned the celebrated
Bowes silver kettle and tripod from Simon Pantin; and
examples of furniture by the best cabinet makers, bought
by Bowes for Gibside, turn up from time to time in the
London sale rooms.

2

The best of everything was just good enough for George
Bowes—and that applied to his properties, his horses, his
coal pits, the fruit and flowers at Gibside, and to everything
that was his. Most of all he wanted the best of everything
for his only child. Writing years later Mary Eleanor Bowes
herself described with what measure of success and failure
this elderly father undertook the supervision of her education.

'I am convinced', she rather sadly confessed, 'that a want
of a proper sense of religion has been the original cause of
all my errors; all the grounds of this mischief were laid before

my father died, and then I was only between eleven and twelve years old. . . . As he was uncommon handsome and a great rake in his youth, he grew very pious in his advanced years, and having felt the want of education and study he was (as I have heard him say) determined his heir should not feel the same inconveniences. Accordingly he brought me up with a view to my being as accomplished at thirteen as his favourite first wife was at that age, in every kind of learning except Latin.

'At four years old I could read uncommonly well and was kept tight to it, made to get many things off by heart. I read the Bible, but at the same time equal or greater pains were taken to instruct me in the mythology of every heathen nation that ever existed; and my father, who was a real patriot and a brave man, was continually expatiating on the patriotic virtues and shining merits of the ancient philosophers and heroes. My mind was so puzzled with such a variety of religions that, except the firm belief of a God, I knew not which of all the modes of worship to adopt from real conviction, as to the weak judgment of a child all appeared equally supported by tradition. However, I saw my father was a christian and a protestant, therefore I called and believed myself one too. . . .

'One other misfortune for me was that, though my father did not applaud suicide and revenge in general terms, by their names, I have often heard him speak highly of men who have been guilty of them, Cato for one instance. My father's whole care and attention was bestowed in the improvement of my knowledge in whatever I showed a genius for, and in acquiring me a good stock of health, hardening and strengthening my constitution by every possible means, often the most rigid ones. My father was continually talking of, and endeavouring to inculcate into me, sentiments of generosity, gratitude, fortitude and duty to himself; and an insatiable thirst for all kinds of knowledge. But I never heard him once say, to the best of my recollection, that chastity, patience and forgiveness of injuries were virtues; and he was very passionate.'

All the Wealth of the North

A melancholy testimonial to the best endeavours of an enlightened eighteenth-century humanist.

3

This then was the background and these were the traditions shared by Mary Eleanor Bowes, by her son and by her grandson.

On the material side—great wealth, which destroyed Mary Eleanor as surely and inevitably as any malignant disease, which enabled her son to enjoy himself according to his own and his period's lights, and which gave her grandson an opportunity of amassing one of the great private art collections of the nineteenth century. Two great properties, Gibside and Streatlam Castle, with their attendant responsibilities and opportunities, neglected by Mary Eleanor, exercised and enjoyed to the full by her son, and conscientiously shouldered by her grandson. And a tradition of zestful living and working which, in Mary Eleanor, turned sour under misfortune, which led her son down roseate paths with no very happy endings, and which was translated by her grandson into a full and oddly patterned career embracing membership of Parliament, winning the Derby four times, owning and managing a theatre in Paris, and founding (with his wife) the Bowes Museum.

On the immaterial side—brains, which all three inherited, Mary Eleanor first cultivating her shining talents and then burying them in the ground, her son not bothering one way or the other, her grandson using his abilities to become one of the foremost men of affairs in the North. Taste, which John Strathmore and his son both exercised to the full. A passionate nature, which contributed to Mary Eleanor's ruin, which would have ruined a less buoyant man than her son, and which was certainly present in her grandson's complex character. And charm, which in Mary Eleanor was dissipated in whimsicality and foolishness, which blossomed in John Strathmore, and which made John Bowes a delightful, if difficult, autocrat.

CHAPTER TWO

Flirtations, Marriage, and
Mr. George Grey

VOLUNTARILY or under duress—it is uncertain which—
Mary Eleanor wrote an account of the young men with
whom she had flirted as a girl, of her engagement and marriage to Lord Strathmore, and of the liaisons in which she
had indulged as a young married woman and as a widow.
The accuracy of these *Confessions* will be discussed in a later
chapter; for present purposes her narrative can be assumed
to provide as true a record as would be given by any woman
who applied herself seriously and candidly to the task of
remembering and recounting her love affairs.

When she was thirteen she met Campbell Scott at a
children's ball given by the Duchess of Northumberland.
Scott, the younger brother of the Duke of Buccleuch, was
then a boy of fifteen.

It is unlikely that Mary Eleanor Bowes was a particularly
pretty child; but she was unusually well educated and intelligent, and intelligence, in the eighteenth century, was
something that even boys and girls accepted, admired and
envied. 'Mr. Campbell Scott', Mary Eleanor wrote, 'liked
my conversation, and as he was smart and clever I liked his.'
And she goes on to explain that theirs would have been a
mere boy and girl flirtation had not her Liddell cousin, a
school fellow of Campbell Scott at Eton, 'teazed us into a
belief that we were in love with each other. Mr. Scott told
me he had a tender affection for me and liked my company
better than any other girl's; at which I was not displeased;

Marriage and Mr. Grey

but, in return, I particularly remember that I made use of
the words "tender esteem for him".'

Later, after Scott had joined his Regiment and before he
was posted to Germany, he asked Mary Eleanor to exchange
rings with him. 'When Mr. Scott gave me the blue ring, I
gave him one my father had given me, exactly the same, by
which means nobody perceived I had got a new ring, and
thus no-one knew but ourselves.'

Even as a child she was not above a little mystification.
'I endeavoured to persuade Mr. Liddell by hints etc. it was
the Duke of Buccleuch and not his brother whom I had a
liking for, and puzzled him, that he sometimes thought the
Duke and sometimes Mr. Scott.'

Twelve months after he had left England Scott died of
smallpox—to Mary Eleanor's deep distress. She kept the
blue ring and often wore it.

Another early 'follower' was Charles James Fox, who was
also at Eton with Liddell and Campbell Scott. 'The present
Mr. Fox had a great liking for me, and followed me, but he
had too much pride to tell me so directly, as he saw I preferred Mr. Scott. For which reason, I know, he abused us
both. But, like Mr. Scott, he was clever.'

In 1761, the year after her husband's death, Mrs. George
Bowes took a house in London, No. 13, Grosvenor Square,
moving two years later to No. 40 in the same Square.
Thereafter Mary Eleanor divided her time between London,
Gibside and St. Paul's Walden, the Gilberts' house in Hertfordshire which her mother had by this time inherited. In
London she was chaperoned by her unmarried aunt, Miss
Jane Bowes, 'who came up to town, and till I was married I
lived chiefly with her. This woman first introduced me to
the world, when my mother could not go out. She had been
a celebrated beauty, and extremely vain; but, unfortunately
for me, of nothing more than having a niece who was one
of the greatest fortunes in England and (although I ought
not to say it, nor do I but with confusion and shame that I
did not employ my talents better) a prodigy of learning.'

She amused herself with 'alternate study and diversion',

having, as she admits, 'an over-desire of learning'. She 'relied on the best masters'; her governess, Mrs. Parish, who had a close family connection with the Natural History Department of the recently founded British Museum in Bloomsbury, encouraged her to specialize in botany; she had a gift for languages and for writing verses; and she enjoyed the approval, friendship and correspondence of Mrs. Montague. She also had a taste for society.

'My aunt', she wrote, 'was so indulgent a chaperone that I must say, if I had not been more prudent than most girls, I might have been less so.'

Prudence hardly distinguished her conduct after she had married, but it would seem that as a girl she was fully to be trusted.

'So great was my reputation in that respect,' she writes, 'that though a young Venetian Marquis, with my mother's acknowledged consent, attended on me for a twelvemonth to all public places as a Cicesbeo, and was frequent in his visits to our house, the world did us justice in believing this connection was entirely owing to my mother.' Mrs. Bowes had a liking for anyone and anything connected with Italy; Mary Eleanor spoke Italian and wished to perfect herself in that language; the Italian Marquis spoke little English and not much more French. The connection was thus profitable to both of them. In due course the young gentleman left London for France—'and so we parted with the same civility and indifference as we met. He sent me two little dogs from Paris; wrote once or twice from France, and once from Petersburgh; since when I have heard nothing of, or from, him.'

George Bowes had left an estate valued at £600,000 in trust for his daughter, who would also inherit St. Paul's Walden and valuable land in Middlesex from her mother. Mary Eleanor was therefore an object of considerable interest to ambitious mothers and to their marriageable sons. Well aware of this situation—she was too intelligent not to have been—she seems to have kept her head remarkably well.

'I had no partiality for any man in the world, though I

had a great many offers made to my mother for me, as I told everybody who offered that I would not hear anything on that subject from any person, as all offers of that kind must come through my mother. Accordingly, they all found themselves obliged to apply to her; by which conduct I was both esteemed an uncommon prudent girl, and had the satisfaction of refusing a great many people of rank in such due form as flattered my vanity and made it impossible they could deny (as they might otherwise) that they had offered to me.'

2

The Lyons and the Bowes' were neighbours in County Durham, for Thomas Lyon, 8th Earl of Strathmore, had married the elder daughter and co-heiress of James Nicholson of West Rainton in the Palatinate. His eldest son John was born in County Durham and spent much of his boyhood there.

On the face of it, John Strathmore was a most suitable match for the heiress to Gibside and Streatlam Castle. He had succeeded his father as the 9th Earl. The Lyon family proudly bore the royal bearings, the tressure, the unicorn and the garlanded girl—memorials of the marriage of Lord Glamis with Jane, daughter of Robert II, the first Stuart King of Scotland. And while the Nicholsons could not claim the same antiquity in County Durham as the Bowes' and the Blakistons, this was amply balanced by the Lyons' royal descent in the female line.

John Strathmore was very good-looking—he was often referred to as 'the beautiful Lord Strathmore'. He had two brothers and four sisters. The brother next to him in age, James Lyon, was in the East India Company's service and was murdered in Patna in 1763. The youngest brother, Thomas Lyon, had inherited the former Nicholson property at Hetton-le-Hole. One sister, Lady Susan Lyon, had married John Lambton, of Lambton Castle. A younger sister,

The Unhappy Countess

Lady Anne, was to marry another Durham man, John Simpson, of Bradley Hall.

'I gave', Mary Eleanor writes, 'some encouragement to Lord Strathmore, but it was slight, though more than to others. He wrote a letter to me with a declaration; and having, as I afterwards found, tried unsuccessfully many ways to get it to me, sent it by Mrs. Baker [a Durham neighbour] who came under a pretence of spending a day or two with my mother who, at that time, hated the sight of her and never asked her to stay all night, as she thought her very officious in speaking much and greatly in praise of Lord Strathmore's family; as my mother thought (though she never positively told me so) I showed more partiality to Lord Strathmore than to any other person. Mrs. Baker took an opportunity when she [Mrs. Bowes] was out of town to give me Lord Strathmore's letter; I guessed what it was but, after reading a few of the first lines, returned it to Mrs. Baker, telling her I would not receive any letters in that manner and I thought the office she had undertaken very unbecoming of her, or any gentlewoman; and that the gentleman whose name I had not looked at or was desirous to know (here she interrupted me and said it was Lord Strathmore) must apply to my mother if he meant to have any answer.

'I left her under great mortification but I did not tell my mother what had passed, from an apprehension it might set her more against my marriage to Lord Strathmore; and because she was so reserved that she did not treat even me with a confidence I think a daughter entitled to. Therefore I never durst open my heart to her, or consult her upon these subjects; and to this I attribute in a great measure the chief of my misfortunes through life.'

The cry from the heart regarding the lack of confidence between mother and daughter was genuine enough. Mary Eleanor was headstrong and wilful. Mrs. Bowes was shy and reserved. This difficult relationship was to lead to disaster.

Soon after the episode of Mrs. Baker and the letter, Lord

Strathmore came over to Gibside in person and 'made his
proposal in form to my mother, who told him she would
acquaint me; and as we were going directly to London, for
which place he was also going to set out, he should have his
answer there. But she did not tell me of his having offered
till two days after he had left the house, and then affected
to mention it as a thing she did not doubt I would refuse, as,
she said, there were three objections: disorder in the family;
a mother and many brothers and sisters; and (the chief with
her) his being a Scotchman.'

If Mary Eleanor had considered that her suitor's proposal
was merely a calculated move in the eighteenth-century
sport of marrying heiresses, it is probable that her mother's
objections might have carried some weight. But, as she
admits, she was swayed by other considerations. 'Lord
Strathmore's beauty, which was then very great, and a
dream, or rather a vision, to which I was foolish enough to
give more credit than it deserved, were two great induce-
ments to me to marry Lord Strathmore.'

The alleged 'disorder in the family', she told her mother,
was a false report, as she had often heard, 'proceeding from
envy, ill nature and partly spite'. The existence of the
Dowager Lady Strathmore and the Lyon brothers and sisters
would give her an opportunity of endearing herself to her
husband, whose relations, she never doubted, would behave
well to her. And the fact that he was a Scotchman was a
positive recommendation, as she had always—a fatal admission in the light of things to come—' had a much greater
partiality for the Scotch and Irish than for the English'.

Her judgment, as far as people were concerned, was always
deplorably bad. 'I told my mother I had no objection to
Lord Strathmore; but that, if hers were insuperable, I would
not marry without her consent—only claimed the privilege
of not marrying at all; which in that case I was determined
to do.'

A wiser mother would have taken this declaration at its
face value. Mrs. Bowes weakly capitulated. 'She then gave
her consent and said she would tell Lord Strathmore when

he came to town, as agreed on; and we went to town directly.'

Family business detained Lord Strathmore in County Durham, and Mrs. Bowes did not choose to send her reply by letter. He, in his turn, did not dare to write. Mary Eleanor considered herself slighted by his silence. 'Though grieved and provoked, I put on a cheerful countenance and danced frequently at Almack's with various people who followed me, though they had not then declared themselves. Amongst the most assiduous were Lord Mount Stuart and Mr. Chaloner. I gave neither of them encouragement; yet they contrived one night to quarrel and put the whole room in an uproar at Almack's about who should sit next to me at supper. Both went out in a passion; a challenge was given, but prevented by one of the gentlemen (I believe Mr. Chaloner, but never could be sure which) asking pardon. Lady Mount Stuart (then Miss Wyndham) sat on one side of me, and having even then a partiality for Lord M.S., begged me to take notice of and manage him, as he was like a madman, and exposed himself to all the company. I confess I did, with a premeditated design, show great civility to Lady Bute [Lord Mount Stuart's mother] and her daughters one night at Almack's in order that, before Lord Strathmore arrived and my engagement to him was known, I might have an opportunity of refusing Lord Mount Stuart. This civility, which Lady Bute construed into encouragement, had the desired effect and, overreaching her great caution and pride, in not offering with a chance of her son's being refused, next morning she waited on my mother to propose for her son and met a mortification which hurt her much and made him keep his bed for a week. This, I confess, was downright girlishness, mischievousness and vanity.'

Lord Strathmore eventually came to London and was told that his proposal had been accepted. Then the negotiations for the marriage settlement were started and took a year and a half to complete. One of the bones of contention was the condition, laid down in George Bowes' will, that

Marriage and Mr. Grey

Mary Eleanor's husband must assume the surname of Bowes. It was while these negotiations were dragging on that Mary Eleanor became convinced that she had accepted the wrong man. 'I found', she writes, 'our tempers, dispositions and turns differed. I wished to retract (and would [have] if I durst have consulted with my mother), but my pride, and sometimes my weakness, would not let me.'

Her mother had been right and so had her governess, Mrs. Parish, who had also 'spoken much against Lord Strathmore'. He was certainly not the right husband for her. Jesse Foot, in his *Lives of Andrew Robinson Bowes, Esq. and the Countess of Strathmore*, writes of him, 'the late Earl of Strathmore was not exactly calculated to make even a good learned woman a pleasing husband. His Lordship's pursuits were always innocent and without the smallest guile, but they were not those of science or any other splendid quality. A sincere friend, a hearty Scotchman and a good bottle companion were parts of his character. He would rather suffer himself than sour the Countess by imposing any restraint upon her.'

It was important that Mary Eleanor should have married a man whom she was capable of loving and admiring and who would have exercised a reasonably strong control over her vagaries. If she had chosen such a man, she would in all probability have enjoyed as happy and successful a life as her circumstances and talents suggested. Instead she drifted into marriage with a man whom she had physically admired but with whom, intellectually, she had nothing in common and who shared none of her tastes.

Mrs. Bowes' dislike of the match did not prevent her giving her daughter an extremely handsome trousseau. There is a copy of *The Schedule of the Wedding Clothes of Miss Bowes, now Countess of Strathmore*, in the Bowes Museum at Barnard Castle. These clothes, it is noted, cost £3,000, and in addition her mother gave her a diamond stomacher which cost £10,000 and other diamonds to the tune of £7,000. She also gave her a green landau, a blue post coach and a stone coloured post chaise, 'which came down from Gibside with her'; and all the plate, linen, household goods, furniture, medals and jewels from Gibside which had not been specifically left to her in her husband's will or ordered to remain at Gibside as heirlooms.

Mary Eleanor married Lord Strathmore in London at the church of St. George's, Hanover Square, on February 24th, 1767, which was her eighteenth birthday. Lord Strathmore was thirty. Immediately after the wedding they went down to St. Paul's Walden.

Lord Strathmore had duly agreed to 'take and use the surname of Bowes next before and in addition to his titles of honour', and had further covenanted that the issue of the marriage 'should use the surname of Bowes in addition to any title of honour to which they might have right'. The five children of the marriage invariably, both in legal documents and in correspondence, used the surname Bowes, and not Bowes Lyon or Lyon Bowes.

After spending a fortnight at St. Paul's Walden, where Mrs. Bowes entertained a large party of guests, Lord and Lady Strathmore went north to Gibside while No. 40, Grosvenor Square, the lease of which Mrs. Bowes had made over to them, was being got ready for their occupation.

Lady Strathmore's health was always affected by her spirits, and it is significant that just before she left for Gibside she fell ill. 'I had begun to feel ill just before I set out,' she writes. 'As two or three of the party had fluxes at St. Paul's Walden, which we attributed to my mother's bad port wine, I said, though I never tasted but one glass of it, that it had also affected me in a most dangerous and poisonous manner by a partial eruption, though I don't believe the doctors were, or could be, imposed on.' This was the start of a painful complaint which was to attack her again and far more severely in the last stormy year of her first marriage.

Her marriage lasted nine years. There were five children —John, born in 1769; George, born in 1771; Thomas, born in 1773; Maria Jane, born in 1768; and Anna Maria, born in 1770.

Marriage and Mr. Grey

In her *Confessions* Lady Strathmore writes: 'I had by him [Lord Strathmore] all my five children; and during that time never had one thought, did one action, or said one word which Heaven might not know without blaming me, or indeed himself; except the dislike I had but too much cause to entertain for Mr. Lyon [the hon. Thomas Lyon, Lord Strathmore's brother].'

This statement, so far as the last month of Lord Strathmore's life is concerned, is not, as we shall see, technically correct; and whether Heaven (or Lord Strathmore) would have blamed her for previously losing her heart to an engaging young Scotsman is a question on which it would be unwise to be dogmatic. But in the main, and considering the morals of the aristocracy in the second half of the eighteenth century, she seems to have behaved reasonably well. Not every wife in the 1770's who was bored by her husband could claim that he was the father of all her younger children.

3

Although she received no encouragement from her husband, Lady Strathmore pursued her botanical studies; and in 1769 she wrote her only published literary effort, a poetical drama in five acts and twenty-five scenes entitled *The Siege of Jerusalem*. Set in Jerusalem and adjacent camps and woods, it is full of star-crossed lovers, women disguised as men, mistaken identities, forewarnings of death, mourning vows, conversions to christianity, suicides, and cravings for 'some convent's gloom'.

Unrequited love is a recurring theme:

> The too short moments spent with Tancred fled
> On downy wings, but left a sting behind,
> Which I attempted not to pluck, or if I did,
> 'Twas with a hand so fearful, that the gentle touch,
> Did only force it further in.—'Twas like
> The tooth of timorous dove who tries

The Unhappy Countess

> To draw the dart the hunter hath infix'd,
> But wanting strength, doth now enlarge the wound,
> Making it wider gape, and bleed the more.

Despite the number of scenes, it is a very short play; and the verse is not particularly happy. Its concluding lines point its moral:

> In Saladin's sad doom we tremble at thy wrath
> And view in him an instance of this truth—
> Nor strength nor treasures to th'unjust avail,
> For soon or late bright virtue must prevail.

Lord Strathmore's lack of interest in culture and in the arts was a cross which she had to bear. She had other crosses, the chief among them, as her mother had predicted, being the attitude of her husband's relations—'the disagreeable behaviour of the rest of the family'. This, she declares, she concealed as much as possible from the world, 'till Thomas Lyon, publicly and causelessly, as many can witness, insulted me in the public rooms in Edinburgh when I was with him and Mrs. Lyon, who was just married, all the race week without Lord Strathmore, during which time he behaved in such a manner as scandalized the whole town of Edinburgh, who at that time hated him as much as they liked and pitied me. I complained mildly to Lord Strathmore about his brother, but it was an unfortunate and most prejudiced rule with him that Mr. Lyon could not err; so I got no other redress than his saying that though he was hasty he had a good heart and never meant to offend. I never complained to my mother on any occasion of Lord Strathmore or his family; but on the contrary expressed an uncommon regard for both, of which she was jealous, and [I] made her believe they used me extremely well; for as I had married him against her advice, my pride would not let me complain had they used me ten times worse.'

The Edinburgh scene must have occurred in 1774. The year before, at Glamis, she had had a mild flirtation with Robert Graham of Fintry, the eldest of three brothers.

Graham, who had been appointed Lord Strathmore's 'game-keeper', or factor, at Glamis, 'with full powers to kill the game, to hunt, and to fish', was strongly attracted to her and she had, up to a point, responded. She hated staying at Glamis where on one occasion she had gone on hunger strike, and Robert Graham's advances must have afforded a welcome distraction. Misunderstanding her attitude, Graham had received a rebuff 'as was proper and which, from my foolish flirting with him, I daresay he did not expect. He went from Glamis in a pet and, being a man of violent resentments . . . he directly proposed to Miss Peggy Mylne, who always had a *penchant* for him but whom he had taken every opportunity both in public and private to abuse in a most groundless and baseless manner.' Robert Graham, who became the friend and patron of Robert Burns, was not lightly to be forgiven.

This was by no means the end of her connection with the Grahams of Fintry. In 1772, when staying with Mrs. Graham, the mother of the three young men, she had encountered the third son of the house, James. 'He was', she writes, 'quite a boy, but a very extraordinary one, and I must confess much too forward for his years, and too conscious of those shining talents which no heart can in some degree, without difficulty, be proof against when he chooses to exert his arts.'

Lady Strathmore had evidently made a deep impression on James's precocious heart. He made a number of un-successful attempts to obtain an invitation to Glamis. 'His family refused to bring him.' In 1775, when his sister, Miss Graham, was staying at the castle, she walked three miles to visit a friend of the family with whom young James happened to be staying. James offered to walk back with her to Glamis. This offer she refused, 'upon which he told her there were droves of horned cattle on the road, as it was the high road to Forfar, where he told her it was market day; and knowing her extreme timidity in that respect he was sure she would not refuse him. She did not, and as he has a consummate assurance and high opinion of himself, though he sometimes affects modesty, he introduced himself to Lord Strathmore and me.'

Having got his foot into Glamis, the self-assured James contrived to stay for a fortnight, 'during which time he did everything to ingratiate himself, and succeeded so well that he could not help perceiving the progress he had made; and indeed, when he pressed me to it, I partly confessed it. Luckily his sister was staying, therefore we were never alone. But us three, walking a whole morning to the amount of several miles measured in the great hall of Glamis, every turn he marked with a pencil. I had my hand on a piece of paper he pinned up at the end of the hall, which paper and pencil —unluckily a very remarkable one—he told me he would preserve with his life; but I hope he has lost it. I am not sure, but I have reason to think he got some of my hair from his sister.'

James Graham was ordered to London to join his regiment. Lady Strathmore was bent on sending him money and 'Miss Graham contrived a way for us to correspond'. A code of initials was devised.

'I received one letter only from him,' Lady Strathmore writes, 'which I burnt to ashes, and drank them up for fear of any accident. I never wrote to him but once, which was in a feigned hand and which none but himself could understand. This was in a cover of his sister's letter, which reached him all torn to pieces and long after the time it ought, so that it was quite unintelligible; and I never after that wrote to him except once, all before he left London. We often sent such messages as we could with safety, through his sister's means, who all the time protested that she would not do such a thing, and made Mrs. Parish believe all the affection was on my side and that she wished to dissuade me from such thoughts and refused to write any messages . . . actually the reverse of her character. Nothing would have induced me to keep up a correspondence or the least acquaintance with her, but my passion for her brother and the use she was to me in it.'

This *affaire* involved Lady Strathmore in a good deal of

JOHN, 9TH. EARL OF STRATHMORE

ST. PAUL'S WALDEN BURY

deception. She had a footman, William Stamp, whose home was in Newcastle upon Tyne. When she knew that a letter was due from Miss Graham she would send Stamp north, under pretence of visiting his family but in reality to pick up the letter, about which he was charged to say nothing.

James Graham, or so Lady Strathmore thought, proved faithless. 'At length,' she writes, 'I thought he used me very ill. I complained of it without redress (though I believe Miss Graham concealed a letter, or more, of mine to him). Finally I wrote a very violent letter to Miss G., full of abuse of her brother, desiring she would retail it to him and adding that he might *"aller se faire pendre"*.'

Miss Graham was bitterly hurt and the correspondence ended. Lady Strathmore continued to seek and obtain news of James Graham and, after Lord Strathmore's death, he called at her house. 'I would not see him. He attempted to throw himself in my way to no purpose.'

By that time she had become involved with another admirer and, as she puts it, 'having at the risk of my life conquered my headstrong passion, I was determined not to expose myself to another conflict with one I had so much reason to be afraid of'. But she could not quite leave James Graham alone. In a postscript to her account of this episode she relates that the second Graham brother, David, had also admired her and that, according to Miss Graham, 'when he spoke of me his eyes used to dart fire and sparkle like diamonds. . . . But I was so taken up with James that I paid no attention to him.' And finally, after admitting to two later and less innocent *affaires*, she writes, 'Mr. James Graham was the only one besides who could have stood the least chance of succeeding in such an attempt. Yet, violent as my passion for him was, I do sincerely think that it was pure, for my anxiety about his health and welfare continued two years after he left England, though I never saw or heard from him during that time or received a message from him by his sister above twice, though she always wrote about him.'

The Unhappy Countess

This episode certainly upset and unsettled Lady Strathmore, whose relations with her husband had become strained. There were faults on both sides. One contributing factor, for which neither party could be blamed, was Lord Strathmore's ill health. He had developed consumption and on his doctor's orders paid long visits to Bristol and Bath, visits on which Lady Strathmore did not accompany him. She remained in London with the children and with her own former governess, Mrs. Parish. Both Lord and Lady Strathmore were extravagant and ran up considerable debts—it was said that Lord Strathmore owed £30,000 when he died. He may have been a gambler, but although he maintained his father-in-law's thoroughbred stud at Streatlam he was not particularly prominent on the Turf. Lady Strathmore's temperament cannot have been an easy one—the rancour which she felt for anyone against whom she had a grievance has been illustrated in the quoted extracts from her *Confessions*. No doubt she harboured a good deal of resentment against her husband. Writing in her *Confessions* of her friendship with Mrs. Montague she comments, 'this continued without interruption till Lord Strathmore, after my marriage, obliged me to break off with her in a very rude and abrupt manner (going no more to her Sundays and only once a year rapping at her door) telling me she was a wild, light, silly woman of bad character and not fit for my acquaintance. Sadly against my inclination I was forced to comply and give her up, with many others.' It must be said in fairness to Lord Strathmore that it was generally accepted at the time that his wife had treated him badly and had hastened his decline. The evidence for this is vague. He accused her of 'folly and extravagance such as the purchase of stuffed animals and other useless and absurd extravagances'. But a mild mania for collecting could hardly have contributed very materially to the total of his own debts. He blamed her for getting on badly with his family —but on her own showing the Lyons had treated her unkindly. He accused her, probably with some justice, of being whimsical and of being ridiculously fond of dogs and cats.

34

He complained that she was indiscreet and was too prone to say clever but wounding things. More seriously, he accused her of favouring her daughters at the expense of her sons. That he had grounds for this last complaint is borne out by the fact that Lady Strathmore begins her *Confessions* with this admission: 'The first [crime], my unnatural dislike to my eldest son, for faults which, at most, he could only be the innocent cause and not the author of. Of this I have repented many months ago and am most sincerely sorry I did not sooner, in compliance with most sincere and disinterested advice.' The most serious charge of all, and one that Lord Strathmore does not seem to have made, was that she had drifted into a liaison with a Mr. George Grey.

4

George Grey (or Gray, the two spellings are used indiscriminately) entered Lady Strathmore's life at a time when she badly needed a friend and confidant; and we may picture him as a fundamentally dishonest, lazy, amorous, literary, greedy, pussy-cat of a man, attentive, good company, and with plenty of time on his hands, but not too lazy or too stupid to constitute a considerable menace to an unhappily married, lonely young woman who had been badly bruised by a frustrating love affair.

The identity of George Grey is a puzzle. In the article on Lady Strathmore in *The Dictionary of National Biography* he is described as 'the hon. George Grey'; but appropriate books of reference fail to disclose any such person. There was a George Grey of Southwick, in County Durham, who married an Ogle of Kirkley and whose daughter married Charles Grey of Howick, later the 1st Earl Grey. But this George Grey died in 1746.

Lady Strathmore's friend remains a mysterious figure and we have to fall back on Jesse Foot's description of him as 'a gentleman from India, who had served under Lord Clive in no very high capacity, but had made a fortune and purchased land in Scotland'. Foot evidently had a poor opinion of him, for he speaks disparagingly of his age, want of spirit, and languor; and this opinion is also reflected in a satirical ballad, *The Stoniad: Addressed to Andrew Robinson*, the manuscript of which is in the Central Library, Newcastle upon Tyne:

> And now to *half-wake* orient Gray we bow,
> Who came from Ganges tout a fait Gentoo.
> He deeply floundering on the when and where,
> Was to his Muzzled Bull Dogs giving Air.
> Struck at the Armament with little Pains,
> We sucked the Mystery from his addl'd Brains.

There was a 'Mr. Gray' who was dismissed in 1765 from the Council of Bengal by Clive, who believed him to have been venal; and the following passage occurs in a letter written by Clive to Harry Verelst from Dum Dumma on January 3rd, 1766; 'On New Year's Day Leicester handed Mrs. Sumner into the Ball Room, sat next to her and danced with her; George Gray as usual with Mrs. Grant, and on the General's public day he sent no excuse that he was engaged, and after having made the General wait for some time he received information the Gentleman was gone to a great chevaux at Mr. Gray's. Birds of a feather will flock together.'

At all events George Grey was in London in 1774 and struck up a friendship with Lady Strathmore. She continues the story in her *Confessions*: 'It was not till after many months of constant attention, and many marks of sincerity and friendship, that just as I was going to St. Paul's Walden for two months [this was in the spring of 1775. Lord Strathmore was drinking the waters at Bristol], Mr. Grey ventured to give me some verses which expressed in a delicate though in too tender a manner for mere friendship his regard for me and his great concern at my leaving London. From many circumstances I had conceived so high an opinion of the goodness of his heart and disposition that I was unwilling to lose his friendship; so that, though I made no answer, I ex-

36

pressed no anger, but continued corresponding with him openly and fairly till we both returned to town.'

On his return from Bristol, Lord Strathmore went to Mr. Palgrave's, where he stayed for some time, and Lady Strathmore remained in London with Mrs. Parish. It was at this time that a number of unrelated circumstances, coming fortuitously together, played into Grey's hand. Lady Strathmore gives an account of the episode.

'The post brought me a letter from Mr. Lyon in which he refused, very uncivilly, to send me a small sum of money I told him I had written for by Lord Strathmore's directions; and another letter from Miss Graham, in which I found she had received a letter from her brother who, as he began to do some time before, never so much as mentioned me but spoke with the highest commendations of a lady at Minorca where he was arrived. As I was full of resentment at Mr. Lyon, and determined never more to think of Mr. James Graham, a servant brought me a letter from Mr. Grey who, by an Enigma, very ingeniously invented, had pitched upon that very day to see how far he might venture. If I was angry, he might have explained it away; but if I understood it, or pretended not to understand it, then he might speak plain. I chose the latter method and, full of resentment, I thought I had revenged myself on others, whilst I was literally on myself, as I felt nothing for Mr. Grey that exceeded friendship or gave me cause to apprehend the consequences of such a connection. I consented to accept the love of a man whom I could always keep within bounds and whom I had conceived such an esteem for that I reckoned his friendship a comfort I should be very sorry to lose. I saw him three times when I knew Mrs. Parish was at the Museum, and met him for a short time, as if by accident, at the Ring, without, I really believe, any suspicion; but as Lord Strathmore was out of town—was expected soon to return—he pressed me to see him oftener at my house and meet him oftener at different places abroad. But this was found impracticable without trusting somebody; and, unfortunately, after taking what we thought all necessary precautions, we

37

The Unhappy Countess

agreed to trust George Walker [her footman] whose secrecy and caution we both thought we had reason to be satisfied with. We imprudently allowed him to tell us freely all the reports of the town, on every occasion where either [of us] were in the least concerned.'

All the ingredients for a public scandal were present; but Lady Strathmore seems to have done her best to lay down conditions for this unwise friendship. 'I told Mr. Grey that he had my friendship and esteem; that my heart had long been in the possession of another [James Graham] from whom I had determined to withdraw it, but had done it so short a time that I should think it an injury against the friendship and confidence he was entitled to if I concealed the circumstance from him. Also, that I had been so unhappy in matrimony that I was determined never to engage myself indissolubly, though I would most faithfully promise, if on these conditions he would be satisfied with my affection, he should have it entire if Lord Strathmore died; that if he recovered he must give me up, and that during my husband's life he must decline all thoughts of me. To all this, with reluctance, and finding me peremptory, he agreed.'

George Walker, on at least one occasion, saved Lady Strathmore from an embarrassing situation 'by a ready turn' when George Grey was in her house. Lord Strathmore came back to London and George Grey went to Bath. Lady Strathmore and Grey had agreed not to correspond until she could write and tell him that the coast was clear and that he could come back. But Grey was impatient and sent her a note saying that he had returned to London without a summons because he had to see her for an hour or two.

They met very early one morning in St. James's Park. It was a freezingly cold day, she slipped on the ice, fell, and cut herself. She did not change her shoes or her petticoat until some time after she had returned home and, as a result, contracted a fever. Lord Strathmore once more went to Bristol, and soon after Lady Strathmore had written to Grey to give him this intelligence she had a serious recurrence of the ague in the face from which she had suffered on her honeymoon. 'My head swelled so,' she writes, 'yet without easing my pain, that I was blind and even spoke with pain.'

Mr. Grey was all attention, 'writing to me all day and sitting by me all evening; and unknown, as I thought, by all but George [Walker] and unsuspected by all but Mrs. Parish, who sometimes remonstrated, but very gently, and I turned it off with a laugh or joke.'

For Lady Strathmore's entertainment George Grey is believed to have written *The Turkish Tale*, a tedious piece, published anonymously, which tells the story of Adam and Eve and a servant called Vixen. It was Vixen, in Grey's version, who gave the apple to Eve.

Lady Strathmore recovered; and Lord Strathmore, in a desperate—and as he probably knew hopeless—bid for health planned to sail for Lisbon, where rich consumptives coughed out their lives in the coffee room of Mrs. Williams's celebrated hotel.

But in the middle of February, 1776, a week or two before husband and wife parted for the last time, George Grey claimed his reward for all his visits and letter-writings. 'One unfortunate evening,' Lady Strathmore confesses, 'I was off my guard, and ever after that I lived occasionally with him as his wife.'

CHAPTER THREE

The Temple of Folly

LORD STRATHMORE died at sea on March 7th, 1776. Lady Strathmore did not receive the news until April 6th, and with it came a letter which her husband had written on board ship. This farewell letter, which Jesse Foot mentions but does not quote, came into the possession of the late Mrs. James Maxtone Graham, who gave a copy of it to the Bowes Museum.

'As this is not intended for your perusal till I am dead I hope you will pay a little more attention to it than you ever did to anything I said to you while alive.

'I do not mean to study elegance, but truth; and to offer you the best advice my experience will afford. In the first place I freely forgive you all your liberties and follies (however fatal they have been to me) as being thoroughly persuaded they were not the produce of your own mind, but the suggestions of some vile interested monster. I next do most solemnly declare (and I write this declaration in a full belief that I have a very short time to live) that I am convinced all the prejudices you have conceived against my family are entirely without foundation, and, as such, I would request you would lay them aside, at least until you have fresh matter or cause for complaint. I must also earnestly desire you would endeavour to give up your foolish partiality for your daughters, and that most unnatural prejudice you have against your eldest innocent son. All children should rank equally in a parent's mind, at least until they have forfeited that regard which was due to them from their birth; favour is commonly more hurtful to the child than the contrary, but either without reason is an infallible mark of the badness of the parent's heart. I will say nothing of your extreme rage for literary fame. I think your own understanding, when matured, will convince you of the futility of the pursuit. I recommend you to give a greater complacency to those with whom you converse, and more candour in giving your opinion of those upon [whom] the conversation happens to fall. Above all, I would wish you to avoid all appearance of malice, and entreat you not to be tempted to say an ill-natured thing for the sake of sporting a *bon mot*. I come now to a point very essential to your ease and comfort, and allow me to say that no one ever studied with more attention to promote the happiness of another than I have constantly done to promote yours. If I have not succeeded it is my misfortune, not my fault. What I mean to speak of relates to your Estate, the management of which, as you have never known about it, it is impossible you should understand. For which reason I would advise you most earnestly to appoint some person you can confide in, to fix with your sons' trustees for a certain sum payable quarterly or half yearly as you shall approve. I do not mean that you should receive less than the value of the Estate, that the person you employ will naturally take care of; but that you will know for certain what you have to receive, and be free from the imposition of Steward, the plague of repairs, and many troubles attending to management of a large Estate. The old Duchess of Portland has at length found this measure necessary, and no one will suspect her of having done it out of favour to her son. Consult whoever you think proper upon the expediency of what I recommend. If by sensible men you are advised against it, I submit; but yet I assure you upon the word of a dying man it is the well-considered advice of as sincere a friend as ever woman had. And remember one circumstance, a dead man can have no interest to mislead, a living man may.'

Whether Lord Strathmore, when he wrote this letter, was aware of his wife's liaison with George Grey is not known. Grey may have been the 'vile interested monster', or Lord

The Unhappy Countess

Strathmore may have been applying this term to another of his wife's friends of whom he disapproved. In any case, the letter cannot have been a pleasant one to receive; and to the author of *The Siege of Jerusalem* the reference to literary ambition may well have been the unkindest cut of all.

As she had never pretended, except perhaps to her mother, that she had been fond of her husband, Lady Strathmore's situation as a widow should have been an enviable one. She was still young and she was extremely rich. Just how rich is a matter for speculation, but shortly after her second marriage William Davies, who knew all about her affairs, estimated her income at between £16,000 and £20,000 a year. She had many intellectual interests which she would now be free to pursue. She could pick up lost friendships and make new ones with the kind of people whom she really liked. And, despite her declared intention of never again 'tying herself indissolubly', she would have every chance of remarrying more successfully.

But, as we have seen, George Grey had become her lover; and this situation destroyed her chances of happiness.

She found herself pregnant by Grey and submitted to the horrors of an induced miscarriage. The Lyon relations, acting in the interests of the five Strathmore children, exercised just the kind of pressure which she most feared and detested. Mrs. Parish, who knew all about Grey and who often went down to St. Paul's Walden, might at any moment disclose the liaison to Mrs. Bowes. She was temporarily embarrassed by her own and by her husband's debts. And in George Grey she found herself tied to an exigent lover.

It would not be true to say that up to the time Lady Strathmore met Andrew Robinson Stoney she was in complete command of herself—a clever cultivated woman who was taken in by a rogue. She had gone to pieces before ever she met Stoney. Stoney was simply the last disastrous character whom she encountered on a road which had been leading downhill for some considerable time.

Like many clever spoilt women she had no judgment whatever when it came to people. She had picked the wrong man to marry. She had fallen in love with the wrong young man. Grey might have been the right friend and confidant for her, but everything points to his having been a wretched, grasping, greedy creature. And the friends with whom she surrounded herself after Lord Strathmore's death, who were always in and out of the house in Grosvenor Square which Foot aptly christened 'The Temple of Folly', were a worthless lot.

She was a serious student of botany, an interest which should have brought her into contact with quiet, well-conducted and respectable fellow enthusiasts. Unhappily this was not the case. Her hobby involved her with a singularly nasty set of people who did her infinite harm.

Mrs. Parish, who combined the rôles of companion to Lady Strathmore and governess to the children, had a brother and a sister, Joseph Planta and Eliza Planta. Joseph Planta was employed in the Natural History Department of the British Museum; and it was Joseph's and Eliza's circle of friends—'the Bloomsbury jilts,' as Foot calls them—who shamelessly battened on Lady Strathmore's hospitality, no doubt flattering her intellectual pretensions by regarding her as their 'patron' and by persuading her that she was conducting a 'salon'. The leader of this 'set' was Dr. Solander, and the hangers-on included a Mr. Magra and a Mr. Matra; Mr. Matra's brother, Captain Matra; and the Rev. Henry Stephens and his brother Captain George Stephens. These were the 'Male Literati' of whom Jesse Foot writes so scathingly.

Daniel Carl Solander was a serious botanist, a notable linguist, and a person of some consequence. Born in Sweden, he had been a favourite pupil of the great Linnaeus, under whose auspices he had come to England as a young man. He had catalogued the British Museum's Natural History collection, introducing the Linnaean system of botanical classification. He had accompanied his friend and patron, Sir Joseph Banks, on his famous voyage with Captain Cook in the *Endeavour*, and in 1773 he had been appointed Keeper of the Natural History Department in which Joseph Planta was working. Dr. Solander's interests were social as well as botanical; and although Sir Joseph Banks was devoted to him, he had a reputation for being pleasure-loving and lazy. Mr. Magra was also a professional botanist. James Mario Matra had sailed as a midshipman in the *Endeavour*, and was to enjoy a brief fame in 1783 when he addressed a plea to the Government for the establishment of a convict settlement in New South Wales.

It was not all loss. Lady Strathmore's botanical interests were genuine and serious and, encouraged by her new friends, she bought Stanley House, Chelsea, where she built conservatories and hot houses for a valuable collection of exotic plants; and with a view to obtaining new and still more exciting rarities she commissioned William Paterson, the botanist and traveller, to collect plants and natural curiosities of every description in the Cape Province and in what Paterson called the Hottentot Country and Caffraria.

Paterson's employment had, incidentally, a curious sequel. William Hickey, the diarist, had first encountered him at the Cape of Good Hope in July, 1777, when the botanist had still been in Lady Strathmore's employment. Three years later, when Hickey took a passage from Cape Town to England in a Dutch Indiaman, Paterson was one of his fellow passengers. Paterson, by this time, was in a desperate situation, for Lady Strathmore, who no longer had control over the disposal of her income, had failed to meet the bills which he had quite legitimately drawn on her. Hickey came to his rescue and was deeply and most entertainingly involved in Paterson's struggles to collect the money which was owing to him.

That Lady Strathmore did not entirely abandon her botanical interests after her second marriage is proved by a letter dated February 26th, 1782, and addressed to Mr. Joplin, head gardener at Gibside. She instructs him to open a parcel of ostrich feathers, sprinkling them with pepper, and concludes: 'Whenever any Mesenbrianthemums blow, Lady Strathmore is to be informed of it, and what species they are of.'

44

But this is looking ahead beyond the dubious set who frequented the Temple of Folly and of whom Mrs. Parish was probably the best of a bad bunch.

Lady Strathmore's relationship with Mrs. Parish is a puzzling one. Mrs. Parish had been her own governess. She had spoken strongly against her pupil's first marriage. Later, she had come back to live at Grosvenor Square, and during Lord Strathmore's long absences she had presumably acted as Lady Strathmore's duenna or chaperone. She had been Miss Graham's confidante during the James Graham episode. She had mildly reproached Lady Strathmore during the early days of her intrigue with George Grey. Lady Strathmore writes in her *Confessions*: 'At first she thought it only a flirtation, and then she said nothing; for there is not, with all her pretended gravity and prudence, so great a coquette, or one so easily flattered, even on her beauty, as she is.' Later, she 'mildly reproached' Lady Strathmore.

After Lord Strathmore's death, the governess found herself in a difficult position. She knew by this time that Lady Strathmore had become Grey's mistress; and pointed and anxious enquiries reached her from two quarters—from Mrs. Bowes at St. Paul's Walden, with whom she was on terms of close friendship, and from the Lyon relations; and the situation can have been rendered no easier by the tactics employed by Lady Strathmore and by George Grey.

Soon after Lord Strathmore's death an attempt was made to bribe the governess. Lady Strathmore writes: 'Mrs. Parish had displeased me so much, and, apt as I am to be imposed on, had shown such proofs of a dirty disinterestedness, that I determined to part with her; but as she had lived with, and partly educated, me so many years, I resolved it should be on good terms. Therefore I resolved to raise £2,000 by any means, the first money I expended. This, I thought, would be sufficient to make her easy in circumstances if she was interested, as I thought her, or, if it was possible I had been mistaken in her character, convince me by her still remaining with me that I had done her injustice. This I concealed from my mother till I put it in execution . . .

The Unhappy Countess

My mother, I believe, did not entertain the most distant thought that she would leave me, except by marrying.'

The £2,000 was raised and handed over, and it was then decided that George Grey should have an interview with the inconvenient but at the same time indispensable governess. Lady Strathmore writes: 'Thinking that she might be of use to me, I consented to his talking to her, and attempting to persuade her to stay with me, as from himself.' At this interview Mrs. Parish behaved 'in a strange manner'.

Mrs. Parish, having got her £2,000, was determined to go; and Lady Strathmore writes, 'she provoked an uninterrupted series of ill-temper, self-interestedness, and ingratitude; with obstinacy, and in many respects a bad method with my children; and I found she misled me and misinformed me in the objects of my charity. In short she was insufferable, else I would have retained her. But as I owe her nothing, and she much to me, I shall say no more about her.'

But before Mrs. Parish left, Lady Strathmore had to take a difficult decision. 'Just before she left me, I went to St. Paul's Walden to tell my mother I was married, that I might get the start of Mrs. Parish who, I was sure, would write to tell her the very day after our parting was agreed on; and who, I believe, had it not been for interested motives, would have told her long before; which I have many reasons to be certain she did not.'

Mrs. Parish left in July or August, 1776. What did Lady Strathmore tell her mother in the course of this interview? Not, presumably, that she was married to George Grey? The terms 'married' and 'engaged' are used very loosely in her *Confessions*, and it can be assumed that she explained that she and George Grey were planning to marry at some time in the future.

At all events, Mrs. Parish quitted Grosvenor Square and her sister, Eliza Planta, was installed in her place.

All this time Lady Strathmore was actively continuing her intrigue with George Grey. 'I saw him only every other night,' she writes. 'It was agreed between us, that by the intervention of one night, we might meet the next with more pleasure and have less chance of being tired of each other. Not to mention that it was often 4 or 5 in the morning before he went away. . . . I saw him some part of every day, or when I did not, by any accident, he never failed writing.'

In August or September (it is not certain which) Lady Strathmore, in St. Paul's Cathedral, formally engaged herself to Grey; and thereafter wore his ring. She writes in her *Confessions*: 'Another crime was plighting myself most solemnly to Mr. Grey, at St. Paul's, to marry none but him.' She reproached herself later on the score of having become formally engaged in a church.

She had submitted to another induced miscarriage. In November she again found herself *enceinte*; and this time, though she tried a number of expedients, they all failed in their purpose.

It was in November, also, that the Rev. Henry Stephens enters the picture. Mr. Stephens, a widower, belonged to the Bloomsbury set. He was a friend of Dr. Solander and of Joseph Planta and, more importantly, he was contemplating marrying Eliza Planta, who persuaded Lady Strathmore to engage him as tutor for the children. Lady Strathmore writes, 'I took him for an honest, blunt man.' On the day she engaged him he showed himself in his true colours, for he informed her—'which I remember greatly prejudiced me in his favour'—that he had debts to the amount of some hundred pounds and that he could not be easy in his mind if he entered into an engagement with Eliza Planta and lived as one of the family without disclosing his situation. 'This,' Lady Strathmore writes, 'together with the affection he took that opportunity of expressing for his last wife, made me rejoice with having met with such a person. I told him, if he made Eliza a good husband, and if he behaved in the manner I had no doubt he would, I would take care he should have no trouble with his debts.'

So this cadging clergyman was added to the household. His brother, George Stephens, became a constant visitor to Grosvenor Square, and with both of them Lady Strathmore was soon on terms of easy, perhaps too easy, familiarity;

The Unhappy Countess

though she subsequently declared that she had written her chaplain only one letter in her life. As it happens, this letter was later produced by Mr. Stephens and quoted in his deposition of evidence against his late employer as showing that she was 'without regard to the principles of religion, decency, or morality'. The letter, which illustrates its writer's inconsequent and rather attractive whimsicality, was written in December, 1776.

> MY DEAR MR. STEPHENS,
>   Being very much indisposed, though thank the Divinity of Pasaphas [a cat] greatly better, and indeed almost well this evening—your wife takes the liberty of sending you a line enclosed—though she cannot boast perfect health.
>   I expect your condolence on the death of my fourth and remaining Bambino [a dog] at Mrs. Moor's, who is gone loaded with mange to Heaven; and I do not doubt there is an incessant scratching of angels, and picking of their wings, which will rather unharmonize the Psalm singing.
>
> Your dutifully affectionate
M. E. Bowes

Eliza Planta, it should be noted, was not then married to Mr. Stephens—another verbal confusion between the matrimonial and the engaged states.

It was round about this time that Lady Strathmore decided that she and George Grey would leave England on the 8th or 10th of the following April, having announced their marriage shortly before that date. Before the baby which she was expecting in August was born, they would actually be married, and they would stay abroad three or four years, visiting France, Italy, Hungary and Bohemia, and perhaps Spain and Portugal. George Walker, her favourite footman, who already spoke a little French, would accompany them as courier.

This was a sensible decision. By the time they returned there would be no awkward questions about the baby's age. What she intended to do with the Strathmore children is not divulged.

While she was making her own matrimonial plans, she lent a hand in another dubious romance.

It seems certain that the projected match between Eliza Planta and the Rev. Henry Stephens was frowned on by Mrs. Parish and by Joseph Planta. A widower clergyman who was in debt was not, on the face of it, a very eligible suitor, and the Plantas may well have had other reasons for disliking him. With characteristic recklessness and, as her *Confessions* suggest, with deliberate malice towards Mrs. Parish, Lady Strathmore, as Christmas approached, gave her chaplain the wherewithal to elope with the governess to Scotland. Lady Strathmore withdrew to St. Paul's Walden until this new storm should have blown over. 'I left George Walker in town,' she writes, 'to receive the Planta family, and to send me a constant account of their motions; which he did.'

But already, in August or September, a new complication had entered Lady Strathmore's already complicated life. She had made the acquaintance of Andrew Robinson Stoney.

2

In 1776 Andrew Robinson Stoney was a half-pay lieutenant in the 30th Regiment which had been disbanded in 1763. He had been promoted Lieutenant in 1770. He liked to be addressed as 'Captain Stoney'. The 30th, a marching regiment, had been stationed at Newcastle upon Tyne and there Stoney had met and married Miss Hannah Newton, daughter of William Newton of Burnopfield, Co. Durham, 'a gentleman concerned in the Newcastle coal trade'. Miss Newton was an heiress with a fortune of between £20,000 and £30,000 and a house and estate near Lanchester, Co. Durham—Cold Pike Hill, generally referred to by Stoney and others as Coal Pig Hill. Bowes, in later years, erroneously described Cold Pike Hill as 'the home of his first wife's ancestors'. It had been bought by the Newtons in the 1740's.

From Stoney's point of view this had been a most useful marriage. The younger son of a respectable family in King's

49

The Unhappy Countess

County, Ireland, he had had no money of his own and his commission in the army had been purchased for him by a kinsman, General Armstrong.

The first Mrs. Stoney, according to Jesse Foot, was short, dark and not at all handsome, but 'bore the character of a very good woman'. The marriage was not a happy one. Mrs. Stoney gave birth to several still-born children. This annoyed Stoney who caused the church bells to be rung in order to suggest, falsely, that one of these infants had been born alive. It would seem that he wished to safeguard his own interest in Cold Pike Hill in the event of his wife predeceasing him. This was quite on the cards, for he seems to have treated her disgracefully. As a friend of the unfortunate Hannah Stoney wrote to Jesse Foot: 'In a short time he broke her heart. He knew secret ways of provoking her before company and then, if she looked displeased, or said anything tart, he appealed to the company.' On one occasion he is said to have pushed her down a flight of stairs and on another to have locked her in a closet barely big enough to hold her, keeping her there for some time and restricting her daily diet to a single egg. This story was widely accepted in county Durham and some added that Mrs. Stoney was wearing only a chemise and others that she was without even this garment.

She died, and Stoney managed to retain both her fortune and Cold Pike Hill.

In 1776, therefore, though his reputation was anything but good, Stoney was a man of some means. Foot describes him as tall, over five feet ten inches. His speech was soft —and it is safe to assume an Irish brogue. His eyes were bright and small and he had a perfect command over them. His eyebrows were low, large and sandy. His hair was light, his smile agreeable, and his wit ready; but, as Foot writes, 'he was always the first to laugh at what he said, which forced others to laugh also'. His conversation was shallow. His education bare. And finally, as the observant Foot noted, 'there was something uncommon in the connection of his nose with his upper lip; he could never talk without the nose, which was long and curved downwards, being also moved ridiculously with the upper lip. . . . It was seen much more in serious discourse than in light conversation. It was when he meant to be emphatic that it was most discovered. In light conversation he avoided it, by not employing the upper lip beyond a certain extent; and in that case he was necessarily forced to lisp.'

During the summer of 1776 Stoney had been dividing his time between the fashionable English watering-places and the petty clubs of St. James's, occupying himself with gaming, cock-fighting and horse-racing. A society in which, as Foot observes, 'all are much upon a level amongst each other, exchange their horses, their dogs and their mistresses for the capricious accommodation of one another; and keep a sharp look out for the opportunity of obtaining money and improving their fortunes from heir or heiress, by play or marriage, no matter which'.

Such was the singularly dangerous rogue who presented himself at Lady Strathmore's house in Grosvenor Square. Burnopfield, where his father-in-law had lived, is close to Gibside. His connection with the Newtons presumably gave him an entrée to Lady Strathmore's house. Unfortunately he was just the kind of third-rate bounder to whom Lady Strathmore would have been attracted. Furthermore he was Irish—and she had a special predilection for Irishmen.

Stoney must have known of Lady Strathmore's liaison with George Grey, for it was the talk of the town. Indeed, Lady Strathmore seems actually to have encouraged publicity. She writes in her *Confessions*; 'I was always extremely silly in not minding reports; on the contrary rather encouraged them; partly that I might laugh at other people's absurdities and credulity, and partly because I left it to time and reason to show they were false, and thought a variety of reports would puzzle people; so that they would look upon every one relating to me as equally false, and even not credit the truth. Whereas I have since had reason to fear it had quite a contrary effect from what I imagined and intended.'

The Unhappy Countess

Lady Strathmore represented just the kind of rich prize that Stoney and his friends would most covet, and he probably wasted no time in deciding to try and wrest her away from George Grey. But at the start his chances must have looked distinctly poor. Grey was her accepted lover and her acknowledged fiancé. She wore his ring. Her mother was apprised of the engagement.

But Stoney was essentially a schemer, and there were certain elements in the situation on which a ruthless man, who was not particular about the methods he employed, could build.

He was dealing, as he must soon have discovered, with a susceptible and extremely credulous young woman; and the Grosvenor Square household presented admirable opportunities for intrigue. The Rev. Henry Stephens was scheming to marry Eliza Planta and would welcome an ally. The Male Literati were susceptible to bribery and flattery. Mrs. Parish and her brother Joseph hated both Henry Stephens and Grey. And Stoney could look for help from another set of allies in a most unexpected quarter. The Lyons were bitterly opposed to Lady Strathmore's projected marriage to George Grey and were prepared to go to considerable lengths to prevent it. Their attitude was understandable. Lord Strathmore had been dead only a few months. A second husband would, on marriage, gain control of Lady Strathmore's fortune. There were the interests of the five children to consider. After Lord Strathmore's death none of the Lyons came to Grosvenor Square, but they must have watched events with an alarmed curiosity.

Finally Stoney possessed certain important advantages over his rival. As Foot puts it, 'he was, in the first place, ten years younger; in the second place more cunning; in the third bred up more regularly to the trade; in the fourth had the superior aid, the air, and the necessary art of a man of the St. James's Coffee House. There was no antiquated, dissipated, impudent and profligate nabob a match for him.'

Later on, Stoney was to prove one of the worst schemers in the world. In his campaign to steal Lady Strathmore from Grey he played his cards with the skill of a practised cheater.

First he enlisted Eliza Planta and Mr. Stephens on his side. Then he gained the support of the rest of the Male Literati. And then he made a direct onslaught on Lady Strathmore's credulity. In October, at the suggestion of Eliza Planta but on the prompting of Stoney, Lady Strathmore was induced to visit the 'Conjuror' in Pear Street.

She was addicted to fortune-tellers. During her husband's lifetime she had consulted one on Ludgate Hill, and had twice visited a woman in Crown Court. And on several occasions she had consulted gipsies near St. Paul's Walden.

On the morning of the Pear Street visit Eliza, Mr. Matra and a shadowy character called Mr. Pennick breakfasted with Lady Strathmore in Grosvenor Square, and Captain Matra met them half way to their destination. On reaching the Old Bailey they were accosted by a small boy who asked them if they wanted the gentleman 'so many people came after'. On being told they did he led them through blind alleys to Pear Street which they reached between eleven and twelve o'clock. The room in which they waited until the 'conjuror' was ready to receive them was the coldest Lady Strathmore had ever encountered, with no furniture except three rotten chairs and a wooden trunk. With difficulty they obtained logs of green wood which they put in a chimney place where there was no grate. They had nothing to eat and they beguiled their wait by writing verses on the wall and by observing the fortune-teller's other clients. Lady Strathmore spoke to the most decent-looking of the waiting women who told her that she repented of not having taken the 'conjuror's' advice which he had given her on a previous occasion, and in return Lady Strathmore informed this complete stranger that she was a grocer's widow who was in doubt as to whether she should marry a Brewer or a Sugar Boiler, both of whom had proposed to her. Lady Strathmore also spoke, in Spanish, to a Portuguese Jewish boy of fifteen whose father, a pawnbroker, had sent him to find out who had stolen some silver spoons.

The Unhappy Countess

It was six o'clock in the evening before it was Lady Strathmore's turn to go down to the cellar room where the 'conjuror' interviewed his clients. She was accompanied by Captain Matra who, she writes, 'went down in perfect unbelief and came up convinced of the man's knowledge from what he told him'.

What the 'conjuror' told Lady Strathmore is not divulged, but Foot is convinced that the man had been primed in advance by Stoney, so he may well have hinted that whereas she was engaged to marry a gentleman who had seen service in India, she would in fact marry a fascinating young Irishman who had recently come into her life.

In December, the pace of Stoney's attack quickened. As a start, Lady Strathmore received through the post what purported to be the copy of a letter written to Stoney by a lady living in Durham to whom he had been paying his addresses. This lady had regarded herself as engaged to Stoney, and the letter was full of reproaches on the score of his having dropped her in favour of the countess. She denounced his faithless vows, his mercenary seductions and his fatal delusions; but the sting came towards the end of the letter where the writer explained that she found her only consolation in the fact that Lady Strathmore must eventually be married to Mr. Grey, thus becoming reconciled to her friends and to her own and her late husband's relations. Mr. Grey, so she had heard, had had interviews with members of the Lyon family and had paid a visit to Mrs. Bowes at St. Paul's Walden. This led the injured lady to suppose that 'everything was now most perfectly adjusted' and that, when Lady Strathmore had been married, she and the countess would no longer be rivals for Stoney's affections.

Foot suggests that Stoney had himself written this letter. It was an ingenious move, calculated at once to excite Lady Strathmore's jealousy and to suggest that Grey had moved over to the enemy's camp. A suitor favoured by the Lyons and by her mother would be much less acceptable than one detested and feared by her late husband's relations.

If, as seems to have been the case, she accepted the Durham lady's letter at its face value, then it is clear that she had already fallen a victim to Stoney's fatal charms. And Stoney must have seen his way clear before him.

Shortly before Christmas, as we have seen, Eliza Planta and Mr. Stephens eloped to Scotland, and Lady Strathmore retreated to St. Paul's Walden. Stoney took the opportunity of her absence to write her a letter.

'Woman's a riddle. I never felt the proverb more than upon the honour of receiving your ladyship's letter. Eliza has, indeed, been playing within the curtain; had I been worthy to have had confidence in this business, I certainly should have advised a double plot. Your journey would have prevented any enquiry after the intention of your fair friend, and I then should have had the happiness of making my consort not only the conversation of the day, but the envy of the world. You draw a flattering picture of Mr. Stephens, was he anything but Eliza's husband I should not be pleased with his trait; but she deserves to be happy; and I hope he is everything she can wish. I always thought that Eliza had a good heart; but she has now convinced us that she has a great mind, above being trammelled by the opinion of guardians, relations or pretended friends. A free choice is happiness; and bliss is the offspring of the mind. Those only possess joy who think they have it; and it signifies little whether we are happy by the forms our connections would prescribe to us or not. I believe it will not be denied that many are miserable, under the opinion of the world of their being very much the contrary.

'You tell me that your good mother (Heaven bless her) is well employed for an old lady; but by the soul of ANGELICA [a cat] you vow, (and I know she was dear to you), that her pursuits do not at this time engage your attention. Now by the living sick JACINTHA [another cat], by everything I have to hope, I swear that I am highly interested in your present thoughts; and were I PROTEUS I would instantly transform myself, to be happy that I was stroked and caressed, like them, by you; and, discovering the secret of your mind, I

55

The Unhappy Countess

might experience what I hope Eliza will never be a stranger to, or be placed beyond the reach of further hope. I am all impatience to see your ladyship; I really cannot wait till Saturday; I must have five minutes chat with you before that time. You will think me whimsical; but upon Thursday next, at one o'clock, I shall be in the garden at Paul's Walden. There is a leaden statue, or there was formerly, and near that spot (for it lives in my remembrance) I shall wait; and can I presume that you will condescend to know the place? Eliza shall be our excuse for this innocent frolic; and the civilities shall never be erased from the remembrance of your faithful, etc.'

Irish blarney could hardly have gone farther; and it is clear that Stoney had decided that Lady Strathmore's aversion for her 'guardians and relations' was a note that could be safely struck time and time again. What happened at the clandestine meeting at St. Paul's Walden is not known; but on her return to London Lady Strathmore found a second letter waiting for her from the injured lady in Durham, this time a letter addressed directly to herself.

Once again Stoney's fiancée, by pouring abuse on her fickle lover, strove to show how much she loved him; and this time she forthrightly attacked her rival. 'And must you who possess all the wealth of the North, think that you have the right of thus defrauding an honest heart, too fatally wounded and devoted, because not from your personal charms or intrinsic worth as one of our unhappy sex you thus lay claim to my prize, but merely because you possess more acres and that you are a countess?'

Having got this off her chest she again urged Lady Strathmore to 'abide by your first love as I do. . . . Cultivate Mr. Grey's affections, because your late Lord's friends and relations will accept of him, as your husband, but not of Captain Stoney. It is impossible that Mr. Grey should keep these secrets from you. Mr. Grey has had the address (which my simple and easy fool could never obtain) of first establishing his pretensions to you upon the confidence and zeal of your late husband's relations and friends, Mr. Lyon,

Mr. and Mrs. Ord and Lady Anne Simpson. It is with their warm approbation that he has wisely made his way to your heart . . .'

It is possible, indeed likely, that by this time George Grey had, in fact, come to terms with the Lyons and with Mrs. Bowes. The signing of the trust deeds, which will be considered in the next chapter, strongly suggests it. But it is also certain that his doom was sealed. Lady Strathmore was evidently head over heels in love with the Irishman, and although she was careful to play along with Grey she must already have decided to be off with her old suitor and on with the new. If this is accepted, it makes the strange story of Stoney's *rencontre* or duel with Parson Bate a great deal easier to understand.

3

Throughout the months of November and December 1776 and in the first weeks of January 1777, Lady Strathmore's conduct was the subject of a spirited correspondence in the columns of *The Morning Post*, a daily newspaper recently started by the Rev. Henry Bate, popularly known as 'Parson Bate' or 'the Fighting Parson'. In this correspondence Lady Strathmore was, in Foot's words, 'abused and vilified, attacked and defended'. The abuse was directed against her impending marriage to George Grey, on the score that it was scandalous that she should be contemplating re-marriage so soon after the death of her first husband. The precedent of Hamlet's mother was freely quoted.

In the eighteenth century gossip about ladies of title was thought to be of interest to the readers of newspapers which had a limited circulation, chiefly in London; and editors had far less cause to fear actions for libel than they have today.

The letters alternately attacking and defending Lady Strathmore were immensely long, full of classical and other allusions and, one would have thought, immensely boring.

Years later, in the course of litigation between Lady

The Unhappy Countess

Strathmore and her second husband, it was stated categorically that Stoney had ingratiated himself into his future wife's favour 'by aspersing her character in the newspapers', and this curious claim was never denied in Court. Foot states 'the noise in the paper, and the mischief, was Stoney's'.

Edward Surtees, in his *Lives of Lord Eldon and Lord Stowell* writes: 'Just before Lady Strathmore's marriage to Stoney some virulent attacks had been made on the Countess in *The Morning Post*; and it has since been assumed that he was the concealed writer of them.'

The implication is clear enough. In collusion with the Editor of *The Morning Post*, Stoney wrote either the letters attacking Lady Strathmore, or the letters defending her, or both. If he was the author of the letters purporting to come from the injured lady in Durham he would have been perfectly capable of writing these newspaper effusions. His was a ready and ingenious pen; and later he was certainly the author of both sides of a lengthy correspondence attacking and defending his own conduct which appeared in *The Universal Register*, a newspaper of which he was part owner.

But why should he have written these letters?

In November and in the first half of December Stoney had only one object in view—to supplant Grey in Lady Strathmore's fickle affections. By Christmas he must have realized that he had achieved that object. In her *Confessions* Lady Strathmore admits that she had surrendered to Stoney before their marriage, and it is probable that this surrender occurred during or soon after the meeting at St. Paul's Walden. From this vantage point Stoney would immediately have moved on to what had always been his ultimate goal—marriage to Lady Strathmore, with the control of her fortune which marriage could alone bring him.

How would the authorship of these letters, the most violent of which appeared in the early weeks of January, 1777, have furthered this end?

Lady Strathmore did not dislike publicity—indeed, the reverse was true. Later on, she was to cut out of the newspapers and paste into an album every kind of villainous

report and story that was printed about her misfortunes—
snippets which most people would have preferred to ignore.
Had she wished to marry Grey, newspaper fuss would hardly
have deterred her. This was a point which Stoney would
have appreciated. And he would have realised, too, that
Grey, who was equally set on marrying the countess, would
not have been put off by a newspaper campaign.

But even someone who would rather have scandalous
things written about them than nothing at all must occasionally welcome flattering words extolling their virtues and
answering their defamers. It is therefore arguable that
Stoney assumed the task of defending Lady Strathmore in
this correspondence, hoping in this way further to ingratiate
himself.

Who, then, was the author of the attacking letters?

Foot, after commenting that 'there has never been an
instance, I will take upon myself to say, of such illiberal
abuse against any person, and any quality, and persevered
in for such a length of time', questions how it happened that
the correspondence in *The Morning Post* should have been
allowed to continue. Why did the Lyons not step in and stop
'this outrage against decency'? He supplies his own answer.
'They, thinking that the abuse was useful to prevent the
union of Grey with the Countess, suffered it to go on without
the least opposition, rather pleased with the treatment she
met; and for this saying I have the authority to tell that the
friend in Palace Yard and myself saw one of these attacks
in manuscript before it was ever sent to the printer.'

The unnamed 'friend in Palace Yard' to whom Foot refers
—he can be identified as Mr. Peter Nicol, of New Palace
Yard, Westminster, for many years first clerk in the Cof-
ferer's Office of His Majesty's Household—was the source
from whom the inquisitive surgeon had obtained all his
information about the Grosvenor Square household before
Lord Strathmore's death. A devoted friend of Lord Strathmore, whom he regarded as his patron, Mr. Nicol disapproved of the goings-on at the Temple of Folly and stopped
visiting Lady Strathmore; but he remained in close touch

The Unhappy Countess

with both Mrs. Bowes at St. Paul's Walden and with the Lyons.

The letter which he and Foot saw in manuscript was one of the series attacking Lady Strathmore, signed by the pseudonym HAMLET. It appeared in the issue of *The Morning Post* dated January 3rd, 1777, and refers in scathing terms to the lack of respect felt by 'the Countess of Grosvenor Square' for the memory of her doting Lord, and to her scandalous neglect of her eldest son.

Foot gives no hint as to the authorship of this letter—surely a point which would have excited his curiosity? If, as he had seemed earlier to have suggested, Stoney was responsible for both sides of the correspondence, how did he and Mr. Nicol come to see this particular letter before its despatch to the printer? Foot at this time did not know Stoney. 'I declare,' he writes, 'I had not even heard his name once mentioned by my friend of Palace Yard. I had heard of no other name as a lover but Grey.'

If, on the other hand, the Lyons had not only allowed the newspaper attacks on Lady Strathmore to continue, but had actually instigated them in the hope that they would prevent her marriage to Grey, then it is quite likely that Mr. Nicol, as an intimate friend of the family, *would* have been shown one of the HAMLET letters in manuscript; and this theory gives rise to some possible speculations as to the identity of 'HAMLET'—some person, it is to be presumed, either employed or encouraged by the Lyons to produce these attacks on Lady Strathmore's conduct.

Internal evidence from the HAMLET letters and from the replies which they evoked (replies which were signed with the pseudonym MONITUS) suggest that 'HAMLET' may have been Joseph Planta and 'MONITUS' Stoney.

In a MONITUS letter which appeared in *The Morning Post* of January 7th, headed 'THE COUNTESS OF STRATHMORE DEFENDED', the opening paragraph gives a broad hint in this direction: 'And always so completely armed are truly virtuous characters that even the strongest oppression will not be able to withstand those convincing proofs of a generous hearted woman, who, from a benevolent disposition of mind, has raised and supported a whole family of ungrateful wretches! indulged their vanity, increased their estate, and made them respectable; who, in return for such favours, now meanly and basely expose every little misconduct of hers in a public print. . . .'

The 'whole family of ungrateful wretches' could well be a reference to the Plantas; and the concluding paragraph of the letter, with its mention of 'Bloomsbury Jilts', bears out this suggestion.

'. . . Had the so much disappointed flight of BLOOMS-BURY JILTS continued in the good graces of her, their kind benefactress, it would have been well for them; but let them be assured, that all their vollies of slander, and every method that iniquity can prompt them to do, will never reinstate them in her benificence or esteem, which retrieved them from that poverty, only known to their kind keeper.'

Joseph Planta and his sister, Mrs. Parish, loathed Grey and would have welcomed any opportunity of spiking his guns. They had every reason, too, for wishing to revenge themselves on Lady Strathmore. Planta would have had plenty of ammunition at his disposal for the composition of these letters, and it is known that he and Mrs. Parish had kept in close touch with the Lyons after Mrs. Parish had left Grosvenor Square.

This vitriolic correspondence continued until it was swamped by the far more sensational story of the duel or *rencontre*.

One version of the duel story follows these lines. Right up to January 13th, the day on which Stoney is supposed to have fought the Parson, Lady Strathmore was still intending to marry George Grey; and indeed on the 9th and 10th of January she had signed two important deeds in expectation of that marriage. But she had been seriously troubled by the attacks on her good name in *The Morning Post* and she had urged her fiancé to challenge the editor. This Grey had refused to do, despite the fact that the attacks were increasing in their intensity and venom. Under the strain of these attacks, so the story goes, and exasperated by Grey's procrastination and lack of courage, Lady Strathmore had been heard to declare to Eliza Planta 'that the man who would call upon the Editor of the Paper and revenge her cause upon him should have both her heart and her hand'. Stoney had then and there challenged Parson Bate; had fought him; had been seriously wounded; and his bravery and suffering had so melted Lady Strathmore's heart that she had thrown Grey over and had married the man who had flown to the defence of her honour.

Foot seems to support the tradition that it was the duel which made Lady Strathmore transfer her allegiance from Grey to Stoney. He writes: 'She seemed, poor silly soul! as if she blessed the duel, and blessed everybody about it, for the sake of the precious prize the contest brought her. She blessed even the sword that was used by Stoney in the duel, took it home with her, and slept with it constantly at the head of her bed all the while she was in Grosvenor Square.'

Another and more widely accepted version of the story (which Foot, as we shall see, denied) is that the duel was a 'put-up job' between Stoney and Parson Bate; that the fight itself was a mere pretence; and that Stoney was not wounded in the course of it.

This was the version put forward by Lady Strathmore's lawyers in the course of subsequent litigation between the countess and her second husband. Twenty years after the event it was stated in Court 'That the Appellant [Stoney] had ingratiated himself into her favour . . . by engaging in a *pretended Duel*, and thereby and otherwise imposing on her credulity, by feigning to have a great regard and affection for her.

'That the Respondent [Lady Strathmore] having, on 16th January, 1777 (sic) received information of the Duel (then supposed to be real) and that the Apellant was mortally wounded and his life in imminent danger, she was prevailed upon on the evening of the day to visit him in his lodgings in *St. James's Street* where he spoke in a very low tone of voice, and affected to be languid and in great torture, yet expressing pleasure at the Respondent's condescension in visiting him, and great anxiety to be united to her in marriage before his Death, which, he said, was fast approaching, and that he did not expect to live twenty-four hours; and adding that if the Respondent would only condescend to marry him he should die happy; and the Respondent, believing the truth of this Representation, and from motives of gratitude and compassion, did thereupon, and not before, and without reflection, and without the advice and knowledge of any of her friends, consent to marry the Appellant; and such marriage was solemnized next morning, the Appellant pursuing his imposition so far as to be carried to the church in a litter.'

Edward Surtees, in his *Lives of Lord Eldon and Lord Stowell*, also accepts this 'pretended duel' theory. '. . . he, according to a preconceived arrangement, called out Bate, the editor, for attacking the immaculate virtue of the lady to whom he was devoted, and then pretended to be wounded in the conflict; having probably given himself a scratch or two in order to act his part the better.'

Again, in a Chancery case in which Lady Strathmore and Stoney were engaged, Mr. Justice Buller stated in his judgment: 'Down to January 16th, Lady Strathmore intended to marry Grey. Till then Stoney may have been a stranger to her. The story of a sham duel is stated in the evidence, and not contradicted.'

In the same Court in the following year Lady Strathmore's counsel stated: 'Knowing that she [Lady Strathmore] was a woman subject to sudden and violent impulses of generosity, he [Stoney] made use of a vile artifice to obtain her by means of a sham duel (for it is in every stage of the case admitted to have been so) with the proprietor of a newspaper that had traduced her.'

Against this popular version of a 'put-up job', a pretended fight, and a 'death-bed' switch from one suitor to another we have to set the consideration that at the time of the duel Lady Strathmore and Stoney were scarcely mere acquaintances—on Lady Strathmore's own admission they were

The Unhappy Countess

lovers; and, still more importantly, we have to set an eye witness account of the event provided by a Mr. Hull, and Jesse Foot's testimony regarding Stoney's wounds.

In the *Gazetteer* of January 24th, 1777, this statement appeared, headed *Salt Office, Wednesday, 3 o'clock* and signed J. Hull:

'The following is what I know of the late affair of honour between Mr. B—— and Captain S——. Being in a room above stairs at the Adelphi Tavern, on Monday evening, the 13th instant, about six o'clock, as I was reading the newspaper, I heard a noise like the report of a pistol, and presently after another. I did not at that instant apprehend it was the discharge of a pistol, but the violent shutting of a door, till some minutes after, when I heard a noise as of two persons fencing. This being so very violent alarmed me, as I thought it impossible to be play, therefore immediately ran down stairs, when I found my fears well founded, for after some time, with the assistance of the waiters, the door was burst open, when upon rushing in I seized upon Captain S——'s sword arm, and immediately threw myself before him, for fear he should receive any further hurt from his antagonist, whom I presently saw was Mr. B——, whose behaviour at that instant convinced me that no further danger was to be apprehended from him. Soon afterwards, therefore, (though with no small difficulty) I prevailed upon Captain S—— to yield me up his sword; and as he at that time seemed to be very weak, I apprehended he was hurt, and upon my examining him I found he was much wounded; I think there were three wounds on his right breast, and one upon his sword arm. Mr. Foot, the surgeon, seemed to think one of the former may be dangerous.

'It was a matter of great surprise to me that one or other of the combatants were not absolutely killed on the spot, as I found them, on my entering, in the dark, the candles having been hewed down, as I suppose, in the engagement. Captain S—— fainted twice, but whether it was from loss of blood (which was considerable) or from the violent agitation of the spirits I am not able to judge. I cannot but observe that Captain S—— was very particular in acquitting Mr. B—— of any ungentlemanlike behaviour during the whole affair, and repeatedly advised him to make his escape in his carriage, for fear of any fatal consequence attending him.'

Mr. Hull, whoever he may have been, might have been bribed by Stoney to sign a false statement. Jesse Foot's testimony, which appeared in the same issue of the *Gazetteer* and which was attested by two other doctors, Dr. John Scott and Sir Caesar Hawkins, can hardly be subject to this suspicion. Had Stoney attempted to suborn him, Foot would gleefully have reported it in his *Lives*. This is Foot's account of what he knew about the *rencontre*:

'It was on Monday evening, on the 13th of January, 1777, that I was called upon by a gentleman whom I personally knew, in great haste, to come to the Adelphi Tavern. The reason, I suppose, why I was picked upon was my vicinity to the spot, as my residence was then in Salisbury Street, which is the nearest street to the Adelphi. I was brought into a room where I saw the editor, Mr. B—— whom I only knew personally, Mr. S—— whom I had never seen before, another stranger, and Doctor Scott, who resided in John Street, Adelphi. Besides a servant, I think these were all the persons I first saw there. S—— was sitting on a chair with his collar unbuttoned, throwing himself back, and was assisted by smelling bottles, and wine and water. He looked very pale and I thought ready to faint. He attracted my attention most; and after speaking to his opponent, and enquiring from himself the nature of his wound, he recommended me to look at S——, as his own was not of this serious importance. This gallant conduct sent me to S——; and upon examination I saw the wound on his right breast, from whence the blood was then trickling. Upon a closer inspection, I saw two wounds upon the substance of the right breast, about four inches distance from each other, in an oblique line with each other. As I was given to understand that swords had been used as well as pistols, and as I saw the swords, one of which had been bent, I never have had any other opinion but that these two wounds on the breast were made by the point of the sword passing in at the one and coming out at the other. There was another wound but not so important. His opponent was also wounded; and by the wound being externally upon the right thigh, it excited considerable pain, from the anatomical nature of the part; and though not dangerous, required rest and care to prevent inflammation.

'After having temporarily applied something to the wounds of both, I went away with S—— in his vis-à-vis, and called on Sir Caesar Hawkins, in Pall Mall, on our way to the St. James's Coffee House, who promised to be there by the time I could prepare the necessary articles for more effectually dressing the wounds. Sir Caesar came to his time; and after examining the wounds with his probe, they were dressed. Sir Caesar saw S—— again the next day, and attended him on with me till the wounds were healed. Sir Caesar also saw Mr. B—— the next day, with me, and I remember particularly seeing Mr. Garrick there, as Mr. B——'s residence then was also in the Adelphi. I did not forget to say that the looking-glass in the room was broken all to pieces, which, I understood, was done by the ball of a pistol.'

Foot notes indignantly that the friends of the late Lord Strathmore and those of Mr. Grey would not permit the report of the *rencontre* as it was given in one of the papers to pass without a criticism upon it in another paper, in which 'too much was attempted to be done away, or, perhaps, this criticism might have been at the time more successful. They not only denied there having been a real duel, but also denied the wounds.'

Foot, in short, suggests that while there *was* a fight and while both parties *were* slightly wounded, the fight could not properly be described as a duel. A duel entails proper organization, a proper space in which to fight and the presence of seconds. The scrap in the Adelphi Tavern was not a duel; it was a *rencontre*.

Why then, it may be asked, did Parson Bate, who had

fought innumerable duels, who was renowned as a dueller, allow himself to take part in this unorthodox scuffle? Had he fallen so low as to accept—as it was suggested at the time —a £200 bribe from Stoney to stage a phoney fight which could pass for Stoney's dishonest purposes as a duel and in which each participant would receive token wounds?

The answer to this question surely turns on the respective characters of the two men. Stoney was to show himself over and over again a schemer, a liar and a cheat, who would go to any lengths to attain his ends; and it is true that in the future, as we shall see, he was frequently to pretend that he was injured or that he was ill in order to obtain a respite or to score a point. But why should Jesse Foot—to say nothing of the other doctors—have perjured himself in print? On balance it would seem overwhelmingly likely that Stoney did receive the wounds that Foot describes.

Parson Bate, who became the Rev. Sir Henry Bate Dudley, Bart., must have been quite the oddest clergyman who ever received a baronetcy and possibly one of the oddest parsons who ever lived. As a newspaper editor he was hardly above reproach, but he was a man of courage. Dr. Johnson said this of him to Boswell, 'Sir, I will not allow this man to have merit. No, Sir; what he has is rather the contrary; I will allow him courage, and on this account we so far give him credit.'

William Hickey relates an anecdote in his *Memoirs* which has some bearing on Parson Bate's character and which may also have some bearing on his *rencontre* with Stoney.

In the summer of 1773 a family party, which included Parson Bate and his sister-in-law Mrs. Hartley, the actress, went to Vauxhall Gardens where they encountered three young men of the haut ton, George Fitzgerald, the Hon. Mr. Littleton and a Mr. Croftes. These three young rips stared rudely in Mrs. Hartley's face and, on Parson Bate politely remonstrating, they repeated their impertinence. A scuffle ensued, cards were exchanged, and Parson Bate promised to meet Croftes the following day at the Turk's Head Coffee House in the Strand, there to arrange a more serious meeting. At this preliminary meeting weapons, time and place for the proposed duel were agreed, and then Fitzgerald, Littleton and 'a person in military dress' came into the room.

'Croftes,' Littleton said, 'what are you about? You can have nothing to do on this occasion,' and, turning to Mr. Bate, he continued, 'Here, sir, is the gentleman with whom you had the *rencontre* last night, Captain Miles, who attends in consequence to demand satisfaction.'

Parson Bate denied having ever seen 'Captain Miles'. Fitzgerald supported Littleton's story; and he and Littleton and Croftes left the room.

'Oh, by Jasus,' the Captain said, 'no time like the present. Here, just where we are.'

'That, sir,' said Bate, 'is impossible. A small room like this is very ill adapted for such a business, besides we have no weapons, at least I have none.'

The Captain thereupon took off his sword, coat and waistcoat and put himself in the attitude of boxing.

'Here's your weapon,' he said, clenching his fists. 'So come on!'

Parson Bate observed that notwithstanding he was himself a clergyman he would chastise him for his impudence and folly. Miles took off his shirt, and they went at it. Despite the fact that Miles was a scientific pugilist, Bate gave him the drubbing of his life.

It subsequently transpired that 'Captain Miles' was Fitzgerald's Irish manservant, a professional boxer, who had been dressed up in regimentals with the object of giving the parson a thrashing.

Bate, then, had his faults, but he was scarcely the kind of man who would have lent himself to the deception that Stoney is supposed to have instigated.

A much more probable explanation suggests itself.

On the day before the *rencontre* Stoney, we know, wrote to Parson Bate asking for an interview, 'as I intend to give every kind of provocation till I can bring you to a proper sense of your conduct'. Bate presumably suggested a meeting at the Adelphi Tavern on the following evening when the time, place and weapons for a duel could be arranged.

What happened is necessarily conjecture, but at this preliminary meeting Stoney, we may presume, produced swords and pistols and insisted on fighting there and then.

If this explanation is accepted the puzzling affair begins to make some sense.

In a proper duel Stoney, who, incidentally, was an arrant coward, would never have stood a chance against so redoubtable and practised an opponent as the Parson. In a small room, and especially after he had been careful 'accidentally' to extinguish the candles, his chances would have been infinitely better, more especially as someone in the tavern, a servant or a guest, would be sure to hear the noise and interrupt the fight.

If that was what really happened it would explain the silence which the Parson subsequently maintained over the whole affair. He had lost his temper; he had fought when he should have refused to fight; he could not deny the squalid *rencontre*; and he preferred to say no more about it.

This interpretation seems still more probable if a further speculation is conceded.

Suppose that, round about Christmas, Lady Strathmore had definitely decided to abandon Grey in favour of Stoney, with whom she had fallen desperately in love. In this event she would have found herself in a remarkably difficult position. Solemn pledges had been exchanged with Grey. Her mother and her friends knew of the engagement. Grey would have been a difficult man to shake off. Stoney must somehow extricate her from this *impasse* with the least possible loss of face and reputation. Stoney would have been happy to oblige. It was just the kind of situation he enjoyed.

There had been these providential attacks in *The Morning Post*. Lady Strathmore, at Stoney's bidding, is instructed to make her 'turbulent priest' appeal. Stoney fights his carefully modified 'duel'. And after the *rencontre* Lady Strathmore plays her appointed part, visiting him in his chambers,

The Unhappy Countess

acceding to his 'dying' request, kissing the sword and hanging it over her bed.

Melodramatic and absurd? These adjectives could well be applied to many of Stoney's subsequent actions; and this ridiculous play-acting would have appealed to the silly side of Lady Strathmore's character. That George Grey knew nothing of this plot is suggested by Foot's statement that Grey called on Stoney on the morning after the duel, shook him heartily by the hand, thanked him, and expressed himself full of gratitude to him. That, before the *rencontre*, Stoney was confident of marrying Lady Strathmore is surely proved by a subsequent statement by Mr. William Davies of Bury Street, St. James's who, in a deposition taken in connection with legal proceedings, swore that he had met Stoney for the first time in a tavern in Bond Street 'a short time before his marriage to Lady Strathmore'. Stoney told him on this occasion that he was going to marry Lady Strathmore and asked him if he would give away the bride. Stoney, supposedly seriously wounded, would hardly have dared to leave his lodging after the *rencontre*. His first meeting with Davies must therefore have occurred before January 13th.

4

Stoney and Lady Strathmore were married by the Rev. Edward Gardener at St. James's Church, Piccadilly, on the morning of January 17th, 1777; and Mr. Davies duly gave the bride away. According to George Walker, the footman, Stoney appeared to be doubled up with pain during the ceremony. Stoney returned from the church to his lodging in St. James's Street, Lady Strathmore accompanying him. She later returned alone to Grosvenor Square.

In accordance with the terms of George Bowes' will, Stoney immediately assumed the surname of Bowes; and it will be as Bowes, or Stoney Bowes (as he was commonly called), that he will feature henceforward in this narrative. Lady Strathmore continued to call herself Lady Strathmore.

CHAPTER FOUR

Stoney Bowes and Lady Strathmore

ON the morning after his wedding Stoney Bowes held a levée in his St. James's Street lodging. He was dressed for the occasion in a new suit of regimentals. Two of his kinsmen, General Robinson of Marlborough Street and General Armstrong of Berners Street, came to congratulate him. Visitors in coaches, on horseback and on foot left cards, which were stacked in the hall. The only Bowes or Strathmore connection who put in an appearance was General Lambton.

Foot, describing the occasion, is at his lugubrious best: 'All was bustle, and there would have been something light and airy, something of felicity in this knight-errant frolick of Fortune, something which, on a superficial mind, would strike the attention as a prosperous and dexterous piece of Romance; but the foundation was not sound; the cause was not good; the prospect was not bright; the background was sombrous; the light had no warmth, it was like the luminous appearance emitted from rotten wood in a dark night; the perfume was not sweet-scented; no bride-maids graced the nuptials; Hymen's torch burnt not clear; and the Countess from henceforth may truly be pronounced DEAD ALIVE.'

Three days later, Bowes wrote a letter to his mother-in-law.

'It is not more my duty, than it is my inclination', he began, 'to remove as far as it comes within my power the uneasiness which the unexpected intelligence to you of my marriage to Lady Strathmore must have occasioned.' After a rather lame apology for his actions, he continues. 'As I could not convey to you the state of mind and honour and

integrity of my intention, which were my chief advocates
with Lady Strathmore, I was under the necessity of violating
a ceremony which my inclinations strongly dictated to me
to comply with, and celebrated a marriage without your
concurrence. . . . I shall study to deserve the honour and un-
limited confidence which has been placed in me, and by an
exact obedience to your inclinations, I shall be happy to
regulate my conduct so as to merit your approbation.'

Mrs. George Bowes, who lived for another four years,
never became reconciled to her son-in-law or to her
daughter's second marriage. She is a shadowy figure whose
generosity is said to have attracted swarms of beggars to St.
Paul's Walden.

Eight days after his wedding Bowes hung up his hat in his
wife's house in Grosvenor Square, where some rather
peculiar things had been happening.

On the evening of her wedding day, after she had returned
from Bowes' lodging, Lady Strathmore had given Eliza
Stephens £1,000; and later that same evening she had been
admonished by Mr. Stephens.

The £1,000 was supposed to represent the money promised
to Mr. Stephens to enable him to pay off his creditors—but
it was handed to his wife and was so much in excess of the
sum allegedly required by the chaplain that it may be
assumed it was a payment for Eliza's assistance in the
romance which had just been concluded; and it may also
have been a bribe to guarantee her silence with regard to
another of Lady Strathmore's secrets.

Mr. Stephens had expostulated with her for marrying
Stoney, and this attitude, as she writes in her *Confessions*,
'pleased and affected me greatly, and moved me to a sincere
sorrow and penitence. I thought it became a clergyman and
an honest one; and I thought him sincere and honest in what
he said, and that he risked his fortune to speak truth.'

Two nights later, when Bowes was still in St. James's
Street and when Eliza Stephens and Mrs. George Stephens
had been despatched to St. Paul's Walden to break the news
of the wedding to Mrs. Bowes, Lady Strathmore had a con-

versation with George Stephens, sitting up with him until two in the morning. George Stephens disagreed with his brother on the propriety of the marriage. Henry, he declared, had spoken like a parson but not like a gentleman of unprejudiced education. He commended the marriage and blamed George Grey.

The Rev. Henry and Mrs. Stephens stayed on in Grosvenor Square in charge of the Strathmore children until April, when a decisive break was to occur in their relations with their patrons and employers.

How the Lyon relations reacted to the wedding is not disclosed. George Grey, as was understandable, cut up very rough indeed. He threatened to bring an action for breach of promise, and was bought off some months later by a payment of £12,000.

Stoney Bowes should now have been a man of very considerable wealth and property, for by marriage he would normally have gained complete control of his wife's fortune. But appearances were deceptive, and four or five days after the wedding he discovered to his disgust that on the 9th and 10th of January Lady Strathmore had executed two deeds under which all the real and personal estate in which she enjoyed a life interest under the terms of her father's will had been conveyed to two trustees—Joshua Peele, her solicitor, and George Stephens—to be held upon trust during her life, whether she remained a widow or re-married, all rents, profits and interest from these trust funds to be paid by the trustees to such person or persons as she should direct. In default of such appointment, the trustees were to pay the same into the hands of Lady Strathmore, 'for her separate and peculiar use and disposal, exclusive of any husband she should thereafter marry with; and wherewith he should not intermeddle, nor should the same be anyways subject or liable to his debts, controul or management'. This Ante-Nuptial Trust (or Indenture of Release, as it was more properly called) contained a clause empowering Lady Strathmore, if she so wished, to revoke the trust and to declare new or other trusts as might seem good to her.

73

The Unhappy Countess

Bowes therefore had no control whatever over his wife's income or estates.

His reactions to this bombshell were predictable. According to George Walker he ordered Lady Strathmore to write a letter at his dictation to Mr. Peele, ordering the solicitor in the most insulting tones to deliver up the settlement deeds and accusing him of imposing on Lady Strathmore by forcing Thomas Lyon's wishes upon her. Mr. Peele refused to deliver up the deeds unless Stoney Bowes, from his own resources, made some settlement or provision for his wife. This Bowes flatly refused to do.

The shock of learning of the Ante-Nuptial Trust caused Bowes to show himself from the start in his true colours. As soon as he had installed himself in his wife's house he gave orders to the servants that any letter arriving for Lady Strathmore must be handed to him in the first instance. A week after the wedding, when Lady Strathmore had ordered a carriage to take her to Stanley House, which she visited three or four times a week in order to inspect her greenhouses, Bowes refused to let her go, telling her she must never again order a carriage without his consent; and thereafter he put a stop, once and for all, to her visiting Stanley House. Ten days after the wedding, Mrs. Bowes, through Mr. Peele, requested that she might have a private interview with her daughter. This request was peremptorily refused by Bowes, who said that his wife might not see her mother alone 'even for five minutes'. At their first dinner party, when Lady Strathmore was speaking to a guest in French, Bowes sent her a message by a servant ordering her to speak in English. He had begun as he meant to go on.

The execution of these deeds, which had so upset Bowes, was to have far-reaching results. When she signed them, Lady Strathmore was ostensibly contemplating marriage with George Grey. That was categorically stated by her lawyers in subsequent litigation; and it was also stated that Grey knew all about the transaction and approved of it. It was also stated on Bowes' behalf—and indeed a whole series of Chancery actions turned on this point—that, on his marriage a week later, he, Bowes, had had no knowledge of the existence of these deeds and that they therefore 'constituted a fraud on him'.

As we have seen, it is more than doubtful whether, on the 9th and 10th of January, when the deeds were signed, Lady Strathmore was in fact still intending to marry George Grey. It is almost certain that she had already made up her mind to marry Stoney.

The most probable explanation for her action in deliberately tying up and safeguarding her fortune is this. The Lyon relations must certainly have been pressing her to make some such settlement in the interests of the children; and having reluctantly accepted her engagement to Grey as a *fait accompli*, they may have obtained Grey's agreement to the transaction. In the ordinary course Lady Strathmore would have indignantly scorned their advice. But she was intending to marry not Grey but Stoney; and she must have been aware that this was a leap in the dark. She knew next to nothing about Stoney—except that she loved him. Deep in her nature some seeds of her father's business caution may have been implanted; and so, without telling Stoney, she signed the deeds—'the effect', as the Lord Chancellor was to suggest twelve years later, 'of a lucid interval, and, if there can be reason in madness, by doing this Lady Strathmore discovered a spark of understanding'.

There were two copies of the deeds, one copy in possession of the solicitors, the other in Lady Strathmore's own keeping. The subsequent history of the duplicate copy is confused, but its story, as far as it is known, goes to bear out the Lord Chancellor's explanation.

In her *Confessions*, Lady Strathmore declares that, two or three days before her marriage to Stoney, she gave the deeds, together with 'a heap of papers and letters and an old lease or two of the house, of little or no consequence' to her footman, George Walker, instructing him to put the lot on the kitchen fire; but that she called the man back and told him, after swearing him to secrecy, to burn only the papers and to keep the deeds. It was not, she explains, that she did not trust Stoney's generosity or honour, nor that she herself had any need or desire for money. But 'it struck me, that having taken such precautions on my children's account (for whom I was answerable, but not for myself) with a man whom I knew I could trust [George Grey], I ought not to be less cautious with one whom I could not be so strongly assured of; but I would not tell you of the paper, lest it should look like mistrust'.

She goes on—and it should be remembered that these *Confessions* were supposedly written for Bowes' eyes alone— 'Early in March, your fondness for my children, and the generosity I thought I discovered in you, on all occasions, relating to pecuniary matters; together with the apparent openness of your temper, which was very bearable until long after that, made me assure myself that I had nothing to fear for my children, and reproach my heart for having ever entertained a shadow of doubt.'

Accordingly, and again this is her version of the story for Bowes' consumption, she instructed George Walker to burn the deeds. She adds that shortly afterwards, at Gibside, she asked Walker if he had burnt them and he replied that he had.

The *Confessions* were written nearly a year after the deeds were supposed to have been burnt; and it would seem either that Lady Strathmore was deliberately deceiving Bowes, or that George Walker, acting on his own initiative, had decided to safeguard his mistress' interests. In any case, to anticipate events, when Walker was later dismissed, he carried the deeds out of the house in the bottom of his own trunk; and although Bowes had searched the trunk these papers had eluded him. On the occasion of the first Chancery action, Bowes wrote to Walker, sending him £10 and asking him to appear for him. Walker 'modestly concealed himself' and wrote asking for more money. The deeds were duly produced, but it was Lady Strathmore's lawyers who received them.

This episode certainly embittered the first months of their marriage, for money was something of which Bowes was inordinately fond; and he was soon to need a great deal of it.

Early in February, 1777, not a month after the wedding, Sir Walter Blackett, one of the two Members of Parliament for the borough of Newcastle upon Tyne, died. Sir Walter had represented Newcastle in the House of Commons since 1734. Known as 'The Patriot' and 'The Father of the Poor' he had been a most generous benefactor to the town. Up to the year 1747, both the Newcastle members had been Tories, but in that year, owing to the great expense of a contested election, a 'compromised election' had been agreed on, and until Sir Walter's death the second member had been a Whig, Mr. Matthew Ridley. Three years before his death Sir Walter Blackett had undergone a change of heart, becoming a supporter of the Court Party; and for this reason, and because of a dispute with the City Corporation over the enclosure of eighty-nine acres of the Town Moor over which the burgesses enjoyed grazing rights, his popularity in certain quarters of the town had dwindled.

Sir Walter had no son; and on his death his nephew, Sir John Trevelyan, who was heir to his Wallington property, came forward as a candidate in his uncle's place.

The Radicals were persuaded to put up Bowes to oppose Trevelyan, with the slogan 'Bowes and Freedom'.

Newcastle upon Tyne was a big independent trading town with an electorate of over two thousand. In such a borough, when every voter was said to have his price, the cost of a contested election could be very great indeed. It was to this expense that Bowes committed himself at a time when he had no claim whatever to a penny of his wife's income.

On Nomination Day Bowes had not yet arrived in Newcastle. Edward Surtees records that 'allowance was made for the duties of a bridegroom', and William Scott, the future Lord Stowell, appeared on the hustings as his friend, and made a speech in his place. Bowes' election address contained a stirring appeal to the electors: 'Oh, break the *closet-combination* of the magistrates and gentry, whose glory

it seems to be to treat their inferiors as slaves.' Sir John
Trevelyan's supporters countered this with the argument
that, should Lady Strathmore die, Bowes 'would go back to
his original insignificancy. Would it be decent . . . to entrust
our rights and properties to a man who, in a few hours, may
find himself divested of the very appearance of an estate?'
Trevelyan, they claimed, 'was an Englishman of a most
antient and most respectable family, possessed of a large
permanent estate.'

Electioneering rapidly developed into a slanging match.
One of Bowes' broadsheets announced that Sir John was 'a
zealous foxhunter, 'tis true, and loves roast beef and claret
as well as any fat headed Country Squire in Zummerset-
zheere—this comprehends the whole of Sir John Trevelyan's
merits . . . You are told by those who canvass for him that
your late member on his death bed recommended Sir John—
is Newcastle, then, to be an *Heir Loom* to Wallington? Or has
Sir Walter in his will *bequeathed You* to his nephew?'

In due course Bowes and Lady Strathmore arrived in
Newcastle to take part in the election. According to Mr.
Montague of Denton Hall, who supported Sir John
Trevelyan, Lady Strathmore could be seen sitting all day in
the window of a public house, 'from whence she sometimes
lets fall some jewels or trinkets, which voters pick up and
then she gives them money for returning them—a new kind
of offering bribes'.

On March 14th Trevelyan polled 1,163 votes and Bowes
1,068; whereupon Bowes presented a petition to the House
of Commons against the return, which was quickly followed
by a counter-petition by Trevelyan.

Among the imposing array of counsel retained by Bowes
were two young north country barristers, John Lee and John
Scott. John Lee, a future Solicitor General, was to appear on
Bowes' behalf on a number of subsequent occasions. John
Scott, later Lord Chancellor Eldon, with his brothers
Henry and William, were already playing quite a large part
in Bowes' life. These three ambitious and clever young men
were the sons of a 'fitter' of Newcastle upon Tyne—one of

the hostmen who owned the Tyne keels and acted for the pit owners in the sale of their coals to the ships' masters. Henry Scott had served as Bowes' agent in the election; William Scott, a Fellow of University College, Oxford, and Camden Reader in Ancient History, had spoken for the absent candidate on Nomination Day; and John Scott, who had very recently been called to the Bar, had earned a welcome fee of two hundred guineas for acting as one of Bowes' election advisers.

At the outset, John Scott had few illusions about his client's petition. 'I think upon the whole,' he wrote to his brother Henry, 'it will not be a void election, but will contribute to establish Bowes' importance very much.' In the event, the Select Committee of the House of Commons found against Bowes, but only by a small majority and after lengthy sessions which were several times adjourned. 'And thus,' John Scott told his brother, 'this vexatious and frivolous petition has proved respectable, though not successful.'

Bowes' petition was dismissed at the beginning of May; and on the first day of that month the Ante-Nuptial deeds had been rescinded; the trusts had been broken; and Bowes had been formally and legally placed in full control of his wife's income and estates.

It was Lady Strathmore's case, in subsequent litigation, that she had been forced to sign the instrument revoking the trusts 'by the terrors of personal violence'—a view that was upheld on two separate occasions by the Court of Common Pleas. Jesse Foot throws some doubt on this, and suggests that although Bowes had been unkind to his wife almost from the day of their marriage, he had stopped short of actual physical cruelty. On the other hand Foot was fully in sympathy with Bowes' desire to gain control of his wife's money. 'It was reasonable and natural', he writes, 'that any man in the character of a husband would get rid of such a settlement if he could.'

To raise the £24,000 that he needed to pay his election expenses and to settle George Grey's claim, Bowes was obliged to grant annuities to the tune of £3,000 per annum for

The Unhappy Countess

Lady Strathmore's life, payable out of the rents and profits of part of the county Durham estates which, for this purpose, were vested in trustees. Bowes also insured his wife's life for large sums—a waste of money, as it proved, as he failed to keep up the premium payments. In all these protracted negotiations, rendered necessary because Lady Strathmore enjoyed only a life-tenancy of her fortune, Bowes relied very largely on the good offices of his friend William Davies who, with Childs Bank, was the recipient of a whole series of bad-tempered letters. Bowes was always in debt and expected his friend and his bankers to supply him with more money, more quickly, than they were either able or willing to do. 'I am now, thank God, so far advanced in my affairs,' he wrote to Davies on one occasion, 'as to have quite discharged my debt to my bankers, whose behaviour has been so very ungentlemanlike and displeasing to me, that I mean to break off all connection with them the moment I can bite, which I expect will be very soon; and till then it will be folly to show my teeth.' These were brave words, for in fact he never did get free of debt for as long as he lived; and William Davies and Childs Bank seem to have been uncommonly forbearing.

His domestic affairs were also in a turmoil. In April the Rev. Henry and Mrs. Stephens had been sent packing from Grosvenor Square. Something of a mystery surrounds their precipitate departure. Lady Strathmore, in her *Confessions*, writes with extreme bitterness both of Eliza, who had been her bosom friend and confidante, and of the chaplain of whom she had thought so highly. 'I can only say it was a diabolical infatuation, and that had I known Mrs. Stephens as I do now, I should not only have entreated you to turn her out of the house directly; and have confessed that such a wretch was not fit to live on the earth.' Of Mr. Stephens she writes: 'I took him for an honest, blunt man. Had I known, I should have thought only with horror of his ever being near my sons or in my house.'

It is significant that in connection with the so-called Adultery Trial which was held some years later both Mr.

and Mrs. Stephens made depositions in support of Bowes and against Lady Strathmore. Some upset of a violent kind had evidently occurred in April, and a possible explanation is that Eliza Stephens had let the cat out of the bag in the matter of George Grey's child, which Lady Strathmore was expecting in the following August. If Lady Strathmore had omitted to inform Bowes either before or at the time of her marriage that she was pregnant, and if Eliza and her husband had subsequently disclosed that they had known about the baby since the previous November, it would explain Lady Strathmore's attitude of hostility; and it would also have provided Bowes with the weapon he needed in order to persuade or force his wife to agree to the revoking of the Ante-Nuptial trust on May 1st.

The advent of this inconvenient baby complicated matters considerably. In mid-May Bowes and his wife left the house in Grosvenor Square and went to live in a rented house in Hammersmith. 'It was a house', Foot writes tactfully, 'that the Magravine of Anspach had left, quite secluded from the busy prying eye of curiosity, and where Bowes might hear the cuckoo . . . without it being unwelcome to the married ear.'

In June and July, while he was living at Hammersmith, Bowes renewed his quarrel with Parson Bate, whom he publicly accused, in talk at the Cocoa Tree Club, of having been 'very short-sighted in their late affair'. Bate was enraged and there was talk of another duel; but the matter was somehow hushed up.

In July Bowes and Lady Strathmore went north to Gibside, accompanied by the Dr. Scott who had been called in to attend to Bowes' wounds at the Adelphi Tavern. Foot has this to say of his professional colleague. 'Dr. Scott resided in the Adelphi, where he had a sort of dispensary; and his wife was a very nice and well-disposed woman. The doctor promised from a certain smartness and plausibility to become a useful instrument to Bowes; the doctor had the honour of being appointed His Physician; he obtained all his confidence; and he was well informed of the Countess's health.'

The Unhappy Countess

In August, Lady Strathmore gave birth to a daughter and, to Bowes' great relief, made a good recovery from her confinement. Her death at this, or at any other time, would have spelled disaster to his financial plans.

At Gibside, Bowes felt able to 'bite'. He cut down a large quantity of timber and was then unable to effect a sale, because no one in the neighbourhood was sufficiently sure of the legality of the proceeding to risk buying it. And his behaviour as a landlord was satirized in the following lines, written by a local versifier:

Her Ladyship's tenants first gained his attention,
Whose treatment was cruel—most shocking to mention;
He rais'd all their rents, which if they could not pay,
He crav'd them, and seized them, then turned them away.
The helpless dependants—the labouring poor,
He removed from their work, or horse-whipp'd from his door.

Free schools he condemn'd, and of course did suppress,
As tending to cause and promote idleness.
The yearly, the weekly, the daily supply,
To Orphans and Widows, he next did deny;
Those acts of benev'lence, whence Gibside was famed,
Are wholly forbidden and must not be NAMED.'

After the birth of the child, who was christened Mary, Bowes and Lady Strathmore remained for some time at Gibside; and in the first days of February, 1778, Lady Strathmore finished writing her *Confessions*—the strange document from which a number of quotations have already been given.

Many of Lady Strathmore's actions are difficult to understand, but the writing of her *Confessions* is perhaps the greatest puzzle of all. Jesse Foot had no difficulty in making up his mind about them. 'They were evidently extorted from her under the tyranny of Bowes,' he writes. 'Not but that they contain among many falsehoods some truths, yet these are scattered and entangled with falsehoods, and when found and separated, like a few grains among much chaff, are not worth the search. The rest of the work, if it were true, is of that vile and abominable nature which will not admit of public inspection.'

Familiarity with the text of the *Confessions*, a familiarity gained by many readings, makes it impossible to agree with Foot's verdict.

Internal evidence suggests that their compilation was occasioned by Lady Strathmore having been caught out by Bowes in some lie or deception. Towards the end of her long narrative she writes: 'I have now fully performed my promise, and I rely on yours to excuse all my faults, except want of veracity, which I am certain you cannot find here, and shall never again, even in the most trifling matter, as I will always rather prefer incurring your more than usual share of dislike to me, than say what's not true.'

High words about her lack of truthfulness may well have led to recriminations about past falsehoods; and Bowes probably revived the old grievance about her deception in the matter of Grey's child. By nature he was suspicious, prying and vindictive. Penitent and exasperated, Lady Strathmore may be pictured as protesting that, once and for all, she would satisfy him by setting out the truth, the whole truth and nothing but the truth about her entire life; and, being of a literary turn, the writing of this long document—it runs to some twelve thousand words—would have presented no great problem to her. Indeed it may have given her a certain creative satisfaction. The act of confession has been known to go to stronger heads than hers. She probably hoped against hope that this bareing of the soul would make for better relations between herself and the man whom she had married for love. There is plenty of evidence in her *Confessions* that she had few illusions left about her husband; but there is also some evidence that she was still in love with him.

If that is accepted, how candid was she in performing her promise? When she actually came to write the *Confessions*, how much did she leave out, how much did she invent or twist?

The Unhappy Countess

A very careful reading of the *Confessions* suggests that in dealing with events up to the point in her life when she decided to break with Grey and to marry Stoney, she did substantially set down the truth. The accounts she gives of her childhood, her education, of her début in society, her courtship, her marriage to Lord Strathmore, her passion for James Graham, and her *affaire* with George Grey are convincing. There is an implicit ring of truth in all these passages. Given a certain character and certain circumstances and a certain environment, this, you feel as you read, is what would have happened. But she evades the issue of why she abandoned Grey for Stoney; she avoids mentioning the duel; and her account—and it is a very brief account—of her married life with Bowes almost certainly includes a number of deliberate suppressions and falsehoods, of which the fate of the duplicate deeds is an example. Her marriage to Stoney was a surrender to physical passion and was founded on lies and deceit. From this point onwards she would have found it difficult to be truthful.

Foot is shocked by 'the vile and abominable nature' of her revelations. It is true that, in describing her relations with Grey, Lady Strathmore writes frankly of matters which are seldom discussed in print. But the *Confessions* were not intended for publication. They were written for her husband's eyes alone; and had she known that Bowes would have them printed—not once but twice—and would offer them for sale to the public at the price of half a crown, no doubt she would have been more reticent.

For the rest, both in their matter and their manner, the *Confessions*, written without any conscious artifice, are very revealing of their writer's character. She starts away methodically, cataloguing first her 'crimes' and then her 'imprudencies'. But then, as she says, 'In the course of this long story, three or four trifling occurrences escaped my memory, so that I cannot place them under the proper heads they belonged to, and now they will appear totally unconnected; but as I profess (and most sincerely) to omit not one circumstance, either material or trifling, and that is the

only merit I pretend or wish for in this narrative, I shall
attend to exactness and not regularity, which you will per-
ceive I have all along too much neglected, having written
things exactly as they presented themselves to my memory.'
As she wrote, new trains of thought, things she had forgotten, after-thoughts, kept on cropping up—and down they
all went in the narrative. It is the most unstudied document
imaginable and it is sometimes difficult to follow in its
rambling inconsequence. If any woman ever revealed herself—gave herself away—on paper, it was Lady Strathmore,
for nearly every page of her *Confessions* exhibits just those
faults which she so clearly perceived in her own character—
a lack of chastity, patience and forgiveness.

Yet, if the *Confessions* had never been written, it would
have been tempting to dismiss her as a worthless character,
little better than Bowes. This 'vile and abominable document', which is neither vile nor abominable but infinitely
saddening and pathetic, shows that until she met first Grey
and then Bowes and was corrupted by her association with
them, she was, potentially, a woman of charm, talent and
sensibility.

The *Confessions* were written early in the month of
February, 1778—not quite a year after her second marriage.
In May, a new and this time elderly chaplain was appointed,
the Rev. Samuel Markham; and from the testimony he gave
in subsequent litigation it is clear that Bowes continued to
behave with his customary rudeness. He was, Mr. Markham
deposed, 'of a very savage and tormenting disposition' and
'put himself into the most violent passions upon the most
frivolous occasions'. Once, when the chaplain said Grace
after dinner and thanked God for his mercies, Bowes said,
'damn your mercies, I want none of them'; on another
occasion, when Bowes thought that Mr. Markham had
stayed too long in the parlour after dinner, he called him a
villain and a rascal, knocked the old man down and struck
him many violent blows. Lady Strathmore, Mr. Markham
declared, 'behaved towards Mr. Bowes in a very obedient,
dutiful manner, rather servile than otherwise'.

The Unhappy Countess

That was how the marriage was working out. Bowes'
temper was becoming worse and Lady Strathmore was
growing more and more frightened of him. She was a woman
who lacked confidence. Bowes sapped the little confidence
she possessed.

Accompanied by Mr. and Mrs. Markham, they went to
Ireland to visit Bowes' family; and one of Bowes' sisters
returned to England with them, staying for more than two
years, until her brother's conduct drove her away.

By the following May, Bowes was short of money again.
He sold Stanley House, Chelsea, where Lady Strathmore had
grown her succulents, and took the family plate into his possession. And then, although he retained Cold Pike Hill, he
bought a house and property on his own account—Benwell
Tower, near Newcastle upon Tyne. The purchase price
paid to Mrs. Adair, heiress of the Shaftos of Benwell and
Wratting Park, Cambridgeshire, was £24,000, Mrs. Adair
retaining all mineral rights. Although Bowes let a good house
go to wrack and ruin, he seems to have had a genuine
affection for the place, for he held on to it through thick and
thin and after his death his executors sold it for £65,000.
He also began to take an interest in racing. The stud at
Streatlam, so successfully conducted by George Bowes, had
been allowed to run down, but Bowes now bought several
horses, including Icelander; and, with his friend the 11th
Duke of Norfolk ('Old Jockey') he was, as he put it, 'in-
fernally bit and bubbled' on the Turf. He succeeded in
getting himself elected High Sheriff of Newcastle and began
to press his claims as a candidate at the forthcoming general
election. To this end he entertained the Newcastle burgesses
at Gibside, where he kept open house. 'His dinners', Foot
writes, 'were good, and his table enriched by massive plate;
but there was always a smack of mean splendour about him,
as he did not purchase one single new carriage, and his
coach horses, originally of high value, were never in good
condition.' Gibside, too, was running down.

The election was held in February, 1780; and despite such
disparaging statements by the other side as 'Can the friends

86

Bowes and Lady Strathmore

of Mr. Bowes, without blushing, compare a *fortune-hunter*, a *Wolf in Sheep's Clothing*, an unprincipled *Mock Patriot* to the Independent, Steady, *Consistent* Delaval', he was returned with Sir Matthew Ridley. It was said that his only reason for standing was an ardent wish to obtain an Irish peerage. His attendance at the House was desultory; and ceased altogether when he discovered that this ambition was not going to be realized.

He quarrelled with his election agent to whom he owed a large sum of money; in fact he owed money all round. In London he gave a few dinners and saw a good deal of John and William Scott. His friendship with the Scott brothers—ambitious, hard-working young barristers (for William, too, had by this time been called to the Bar)—may at first sight seem odd. But Edward Surtees in his *Lives of Lord Eldon and Lord Stowell* explains that the Scotts felt something like 'the transmitted claim of family retainership' towards Lady Strathmore's husband. Their grandfather had been a humble clerk to a 'fitter', and their father had made his modest fortune 'fitting' the coal from the Gibside collieries.

William Scott was a friend of Dr. Johnson. In 1773 he had accompanied the Doctor on his trip from Newcastle to Edinburgh; and in 1778 he had been elected a member of the Literary Club. Whether he introduced his friend Bowes to this circle, and, if he did, how Bowes was received, is not recorded. But even the Scotts found their patron rather trying. John Scott wrote to his brother Henry: 'I see your friend Bowes very often, but I dare not dine with him more than once in three months, as there is no getting away before midnight; and indeed one is sure to be in a condition in which no man would wish to be in the streets.'

In January, 1781, Mrs. Bowes died, leaving her St. Paul's Walden property to her daughter. Bowes was characteristically unkind to his wife on the occasion of her mother's death, but he found St. Paul's Walden a useful hide-out from his creditors, for he did not feel safe in London and until his Newcastle election debts were paid he did not dare to show his face in the north. Streatlam Castle was deserted

The Unhappy Countess

and fast falling into decay and ruin. On May 8th, 1782, Lady Strathmore gave birth to a son—William Johnstone Bowes.

Bowes' behaviour was growing more and more outrageous. One cold stormy night at St. Paul's Walden he stood outside the house watching the bedroom of a maid servant whom he had tried unsuccessfully to seduce. Unknown to Bowes, she was married to one of the men servants and in due course Bowes saw the man join her in the bedroom. As soon as their light was put out he thundered on the door and turned them both out of doors. Finding next morning that they had been given shelter in the lodge, he dismissed the porter. The chaplain was ill; but Bowes regaled him with the story. 'And did you so?' the old man demanded. 'You who would have ruined her yourself. You shall not turn *me* out, I will be gone directly.' Bowes would not let the chaplain have his possessions until a constable had been called in.

In the following year, Foot was invited down to Hertfordshire. Among the guests whom Bowes entertained to dinner while he was there was the daughter of one of his tenant farmers; and after dinner the girl's mother and sister came up to the house and Bowes insisted that they should drink tea with his wife. 'When the company was gone,' Foot writes, 'Bowes asked me to walk out with him. He took me to the farm and peeped into the windows where they were all sitting and preparing for bed. Everything, in their innocent custom, was undoing. The dog barked, and I returned and left him there, where he was for a long time. He told me there was no danger from the dog, as he had made the farmer tie him up, because, as he said, he had been caught killing some of his own sheep. He went thus to the window almost every night. In a week after my return to London he sent for me in haste, as he had met with an accident. The farmer, finding that his dog barked thus every night, suspected thieves and determined to let him loose; and the dog, revenging himself against Bowes in one of these excursions, fastened upon his leg, and bit it severely.'

It was small wonder that, on this second visit, Foot found

88

Bowes and Lady Strathmore

Lady Strathmore 'wonderfully ALTERED and DEJECTED. She was pale and nervous, and her under-jaw constantly moved from side to side. If she said anything, she looked at Bowes first. If she was asked to drink a glass of wine, she took his intelligence before she answered. She sat but a short time at dinner, and then was out of my sight. I did get one morning's walk with her . . . into the once beautiful pleasure garden where, in spite of the ruinous state of it, much was left for admiration; because the taste that gave it a creation was not yet totally obliterated. The Countess pointed out to us the concern she had formerly taken in the shrubs, the flower beds, the alcoves and the walks of this most delectable recess. She even pointed out the assistance her own hand had lent to individual articles. In observing her during her conversation, the agitation of her mind was apparent by its action on her mouth. She would look for some time, hesitate, and then her underjaw would act in that convulsive manner, which absolutely explained her state of melancholy remembrance beyond all other proofs abstracted knowledge could confirm or technical teachers could demonstrate.'

Bowes could not let women alone; and he did not confine his attention to farmers' daughters. He got William's wet nurse, Mrs. Houghton, with child; and he raped Dorothy Stevenson, the nursery maid. Stevenson was later to depose that Bowes was 'cross and cruel' to Lady Strathmore and refused her decent clothes, so that often she had 'scarcely a shift or a pair of stockings to put on'.

Bowes' refusal to allow his wife to buy suitable clothes was a grievance which was to be frequently raised; and in fairness to Bowes it must be admitted that Lady Strathmore's daughters subsequently testified that their mother took no interest in dress and was inclined to be slovenly.

But Bowes, by this time, had also begun to practise physical cruelty. Dorothy Stevenson deposed that he gave Lady Strathmore 'many violent blows on her face, head, and other parts of her body; he often kicked her and sometimes pinched her ears nearly through'. On one occasion, at dinner, he threw a dish of hot potatoes at his wife, and then made her eat potatoes until she was sick, throwing a glass of wine in her face 'to wash the potatoes off'.

Elizabeth Waite, who replaced Dorothy Stevenson, fared no better than her predecessor. Her father was in the King's Bench prison, and Bowes ingratiated himself by promising to pay his debts and obtain his release. He raped her; she fled from the house; and ended up in the Magdalen Hospital in St. George's Fields.

No servant girl was safe in Bowes' house. Lady Strathmore, and well she must have known it, had got a very bad bargain.

2

What, in the meantime, had happened to the five children by Lady Strathmore's first marriage?

From a letter written by Bowes to the Rev. Henry Stephens 'in or about the month of February, 1777'—Mr. Stephens produced this letter in the course of subsequent proceedings in the Ecclesiastical Courts as evidence of Bowes' affection for his step-children—it is clear that for a month or two after the sudden wedding some if not all the children were living in their mother's house in Grosvenor Square in the Stephens' care.

Bowes wrote from Gibside: 'I shall take it as a particular favour if you'll show the bearer, Mr. Scott, every civility in your power. I wish him to see the children, as I have the greatest confidence in every intimation that he may give, either in regard to their education, or anything else he may, with your concurrence, esteem necessary.'

The five children, at this time, were all under the age of ten; and the Lyons could hardly have regarded the dubious chaplain and his wife as suitable people in whose care they should be left. It is probable that the foreshadowed visit by William Scott was designed to meet remonstrances and enquiries voiced by Mr. Thomas Lyon and by his sister, Lady Anne Simpson.

The next we hear of the children is that John Strathmore and his brother George were boarders at a private school at

Neasden in Middlesex; and that the two girls, Lady Maria
Jane and Lady Anna Maria, were boarders at a school in
Queen Square, London, kept by Mesdames Carlisle and
Este.

In the meantime their Lyon relations had not been idle.
It can be assumed that their interest in the 9th Earl's
children sprang primarily from family affection or, if not
from affection, at least from a feeling of family solidarity.
But they were also determined, and quite rightly determined,
to safeguard the children's financial interests. No doubt they
regarded Bowes as a crook who would dissipate as much of
his wife's fortune as her life-tenancy permitted. In December,
1780, Thomas Lyon, on the children's behalf, issued a Bill
of Complaint against Mrs. Bowes, Lady Strathmore and
Stoney Bowes in the matter of the 9th Earl's marriage settlement; and shortly afterwards he succeeded in getting the
children made Wards in Chancery. From this point onwards
their interests were in the hands of the Lord Chancellor,
who appointed Thomas Lyon and an Edinburgh lawyer as
their guardians.

Foot declares that the two little boys were never visited at
their school, either by Lady Strathmore or by their step-
father. But Lady Strathmore was genuinely attached to her
daughters, who, in their turn, seem to have been quite fond
of Bowes. At the Bowes Museum there is a letter from Lady
Maria to her mother, written from Queen Square and dated
May 12th, 1784:

'I hope my dear Papa and Mama will not disapprove of
my spending the Whitsuntide holidays with them. We break
up on the 27th of this month, and as almost all the ladies are
to go home I think that Papa and you will not object to my
having the same pleasure. We have had two balls which
I liked very much. I did not dance, as I have not learned
long enough to dare before so much company . . . I wish
much to know that you and Papa are well and that I may
have the pleasure of spending the holiday at home. My
sister desires her duty.'

It would appear from the events that followed that the

guardians not only stepped in to prevent Lady Maria from spending her holidays at Grosvenor Square, but removed her from school before the end of the term and installed her in her aunt's house in Harley Street.

Certainly both Lady Strathmore and Bowes resented the guardians' attitude. On two occasions they had applied to the Lord Chancellor for redress, Bowes declaring that his wife was pining for the society of her children and that her health was suffering from the unnatural and inhuman separation. But the Lord Chancellor had been adamant. The removal of Maria Jane to Lady Anne Simpson's house was the last straw.

On May 21st, Lady Strathmore wrote two letters at Bowes' dictation. One was to Mrs. Carlisle, Lady Anna's school mistress, informing her that she would send for her younger daughter on the following day as she was about to go to Bath and wished to see the girl before she left London; the other, asking that the elder girl should be allowed to visit her, was addressed to Lady Anne Simpson.

Next morning Mr. and Mrs. Reynett, the reigning chaplain and his wife, arrived at Mrs. Carlisle's school, collected Lady Anna, and brought her home. Later that same day, as the elder girl, escorted by Mrs. John Ord, Lady Anne Simpson's sister-in-law, drove up to her mother's house, she put her companion on her guard by pointing to her younger sister who was looking out of an upstairs window.

Mrs. Ord and her charge—Lady Maria was sixteen— were shown into a drawing-room and were received by Mrs. Reynett. Lady Strathmore came in a few minutes later. Mrs. Ord asked if the younger girl was in the house and Lady Strathmore admitted that she was.

After a quarter of an hour's conversation, Lady Strathmore suggested that Maria should go with her into the next room as she wanted to show her a letter from John Strathmore; and Mrs. Ord was left with Mrs. Reynett and with William Davies, Bowes' friend, who was paying one of his frequent visits to Grosvenor Square. After some considerable time Mrs. Ord rang the bell and asked the servant to tell

Bowes and Lady Strathmore

Lady Maria that the time had come for them to leave. The servant returned with the message that she was coming presently. Mrs. Ord waited, rang again, and gave the servant the same message. This time, as she received no answer, she requested Mrs. Reynett to tell the girl that she wished to return to Harley Street and was waiting for her. Mrs. Reynett came back to the drawing-room saying that she did not dare to go into Lady Strathmore's dressing-room to deliver this ultimatum. Whereupon Mrs. Ord asked her to show her where the room was, as she would go herself.

The dressing-room gave on to the backstairs. Mrs. Ord tried the door and found it locked. When she had returned to the drawing-room, agitated and alarmed, a footman brought her this letter from Lady Strathmore.

MADAM,

As you have accompanied Lady Maria upon the present as well as a former occasion, on both of which I strenuously requested to see my daughter BY HERSELF, I conclude that you have some written orders for that purpose from a majority of her guardians; if thus authorized, I should not chuse to interfere in regard to her returning to you today. But if you cannot produce such sanction, you will, I hope, excuse my detaining her till, by representing my case and laying my grievance before my Lord Chancellor, I shall be honoured by his Lordship's command.

However inhuman may be the BEHAVIOUR I have experienced from those who never paid the slightest intentions to my feelings as a mother, and whose professed regard for my children ought to have taught them a very different lesson; yet I hope you will be so obliging as to believe that nothing can be further from my wishes than to treat you with the most distant degree of impoliteness, especially in my own house; but that goodness of heart that I have the pleasure to know you possess will, I doubt not, fully excuse the liberty I now take, and lead you to sympathize in the sufferings of a parent whose children have, for many years, been entirely secluded from her sight, an affliction which, though you have never been so unfortunate as to experience, yet you may easily conceive

93

the severity of; and from your own sensations upon inferior occasions, will form a just idea how impossible it must be ever to exist under such cruel and unnatural controul.

Mrs. Ord's position was an unenviable one. She was responsible to her sister-in-law for the girl's safe return, and Lady Anne Simpson was a formidable character. As soon as she had read this letter she at once despatched it to her husband by the hand of her own footman, with a message to John Ord asking him to join her in Grosvenor Square as soon as possible. She then told Mrs. Reynett that she would stay where she was until Lady Maria was delivered to her, and that she was confident that Bowes and Lady Strathmore would not dare to detain her. For the last time she ordered Mrs. Reynett to bring the girl to her in the drawing-room. Mrs. Reynett returned saying she could find none of the family and did not know where they had gone. Mrs. Ord rang for her own coachman, intending to ask him if he had seen a carriage drive away from the door. The servant declared that the coachman was no longer waiting, whereupon Mrs. Ord, exasperated and sensing a conspiracy, went back to Lady Strathmore's dressing-room. This time the door was open, but as she was entering it was shut in her face by someone inside the room. On hearing Maria scream, Mrs. Ord called out, 'Maria! I shall not quit the house till you come to me.'

Mrs. Ord now demanded a chair and sat herself down on the backstairs by the dressing-room door, a course of action that produced results, for shortly afterwards Maria and Mr. Davies came down the front stairs. Mrs. Ord and the girl were both profuse in their thanks to Mr. Davies; and on finding that her coach had, in fact, been sent away on Bowes' orders, they walked the short distance to a friend's house in Lower Grosvenor Street where Maria told her that, while she had been 'in custody', both Bowes and her mother had done their best to persuade her to leave her aunt's house and to come and live with them.

Anna, the younger girl, was less fortunate; and that evening Mr. and Mrs. Reynett, instead of taking the child back to her school in Queen Square, delivered this letter to her school mistress.

LADIES,

I take this method to acquaint you that in compliance with Lady Anna's affectionate and dutiful request of spending the ensuing holidays with me, I have gratified our mutual wishes by taking her into my possession, as the only means to make myself some recompense for what I have endured for several years from Mr. Lyon's constantly refusing me the company of my children in such a manner as humanity and propriety seem to demand.

I should not have taken this step before the appointed day of breaking up, had I not concluded that if I waited till then I should be prevented, as I have hitherto frequently been, by your adhering to Mr. Lyon's orders; which, however, I doubt not, were highly repugnant to your own wishes and very disconsonant . . . to those sentiments of duty towards a parent which I am convinced you would otherwise have been anxious to instil into the minds of your pupils, and my daughters.

Mrs. Reynett, when she handed this letter to Mrs. Carlisle, gave the school mistress to understand that Bowes, Lady Strathmore and Lady Anna had left Grosvenor Square during the day in a hackney coach for an unknown destination. Mrs. Carlisle, alarmed by this intelligence, called at Grosvenor Square several times that evening and again on the following day, but could get no satisfaction either from the Reynetts or from Bowes' servants.

Four days later formal application was made to the Lord Chancellor by the guardians to have the person of Lady Anna Bowes delivered over to them; but by that time Bowes, Lady Strathmore, Lady Anna and Mrs. Morgan, Lady Strathmore's maid, were in France. Mrs. Reynett had spoken the truth when she told Mrs. Carlisle that the whole party had decamped. They must have set out for Dover soon after Mrs. Ord and Lady Maria had left the house.

On June 1st, Bowes, writing from the Hotel Luxembourg, Paris, addressed the first of a new series of letters to his

The Unhappy Countess

friend, William Davies. This time, his object was not to raise money, but to marshal some kind of a defence. By kidnapping a ward in Chancery and by taking her overseas, he had committed a serious offence in the eyes of the law; and very well he knew it. Characteristically, having committed himself to a rash course of action, he was now extremely frightened of the consequences.

In this first letter, after some bluster directed against Mr. Thomas Lyon—'the other guardian I consider merely as a tool, and Mr. Ord the commander-in-chief. I am now extremely sorry I did not turn Mrs. Ord out of the house and detain Lady Maria. I will make John Ord pay for this insolence the first moment I meet him, let my friends think what they may of the PRUDENCE of such a step'—he makes it clear that he is pinning his hopes on two people to get him out of the mess. One was his respectable friend, William Scott, who had been practising in the Ecclesiastical and Admiralty Courts since 1780; the other was Dr. Scott, the doctor whom he had appointed as 'His Physician'. William Scott was not only to advise him on the legal position, but was also to write a letter justifying the course that he and Lady Strathmore had taken, which Bowes could show to—among others—the British Ambassador in Paris. Dr. Scott was to testify that Lady Strathmore's health had suffered by reason of her enforced separation from her children. 'Tell Dr. Scott', he wrote, 'that I will meet him in any part of France.

Lady Strathmore's health was very far from good; but for that Bowes was largely to blame. When Mrs. Morgan, the maid, helped her mistress to undress at Dessein's Calais hostelry, the Lion d'Or, after they had crossed the Channel, she observed a large black mark, as big as her own hand, on Lady Strathmore's upper arm. The Countess pretended that she had bruised herself in the coach driving down to Dover. In the course of the journey to Paris Bowes, again according to Mrs. Morgan, slyly pinched and kicked his wife and prevented her from looking out of the window by drawing up the blind. He was extremely frightened of anyone recognizing the party.

Bowes and Lady Strathmore

As Bowes' alarm grew, so did his insistence on mobilizing all possible help.

Reynett, the chaplain—'a blundering poor fellow, that would do all in his power to serve us, but he has no head. However there is one good thing which is that he has always been kept in the dark in every essential that concerned Lady Strathmore's children, and his wife equally so'—was to be prepared to testify regarding Lady Strathmore's health. There was a danger, however, that, despite all the precautions that had been taken, the chaplain might be in possession of some inconvenient pieces of knowledge. 'The paper Reynett mentions SHALL be destroyed,' Bowes wrote to Davies. 'Therefore tell him to stick to what he said to Mr. Scott. . . . It will be prudent, lest they should be examined, for you to be as little communicative to them as possible; for if they say anything, they will likely say too much.'

John Hunter, the famous surgeon, whose wife had been a friend of Lady Strathmore when she had frequented Mrs. Montague's house, 'would be a very useful assistant in this business, if a Scotchman would speak the truth against the wishes of those of his own Kingdom'. Mr. John Lee, the barrister, 'will, I am sure, be a sincere and able advocate'; while William Scott's 'abilities zeal and knowledge of Lady Strathmore's oppression will go hand in hand to counteract these insidious plans which have been framed for her destruction'.

By July 26th Bowes was getting restless at 'Mr. Scott's unaccountable and unexpected silence'; and his enquiries as to what was happening in the matter of the pending Chancery Court proceedings became insistent. 'Whatever may be the event on the determination of the Chancellor respecting Lady Strathmore's children,' he wrote to Davies, 'I am resolved to return to England directly after it, though I am equally resolved to permit Lady Strathmore and her daughter to do exactly as their own wishes may happen to dictate. They wish, I believe, to remain in their present asylum. I beg you will have a full account of the trial published in ALL THE PAPERS the day it is over. Whatever may be decided in obedience to the laws of England, I am certain that every feeling and IMPARTIAL mind will acquit Lady Strathmore and will, all circumstances considered, do me that justice which I think my conduct towards Lady Strathmore and her children deserves. Pray have constant paragraphs inserted relative to Mr. Lyon's conduct. I will be answerable to them all. . . .'

Brave words again! But Bowes' behaviour to his wife in Paris does not seem to have been so high-minded and chivalrous as the tone of his letters suggests. One day, at the Hotel Luxembourg, Mrs. Morgan found her mistress crying. Her face and her sleeve were bloody, and she was trying to staunch a wound with her handkerchief. Bowes explained that her ladyship had allowed the wind to blow one of the doors open on to her and had run a black pin into her ear. But Mrs. Morgan noticed that the flesh behind the ear was torn, as if by someone's nails, and that there were black marks on her arms as if she had been badly pinched or bruised. Later, Lady Strathmore admitted to her maid that Bowes had inflicted these hurts, because she had wanted to look out of the window. Not for the last time, she was being held prisoner by her husband. When he allowed her out, he pinched her because she would not wear her bonnet low enough over her face; and once he beat her because she refused to translate into French a letter which he wished to send to a Parisian lady whom he had met and admired.

In a letter to William Davies dated August 9th, after complaining again of William Scott's unaccountable silence —'Lady Strathmore and I have written eleven different letters to Mr. Scott since we left England . . . we have never received a letter from him but one while at Calais'—Bowes writes, 'The guardians, through Lord Caermarthen, have made application to the Court of France to have the young lady taken up. I took care to have timely information and shall, I hope, prevent their success. . . . It was cruel that my friends in England were not more upon their guard. They [the guardians] represent the child as taken off under

Bowes and Lady Strathmore

thirteen years of age, for the purpose of getting her married to some IMPROPER PERSON, unknown to them. . . .'

It was now Mr. Davies' turn to voice complaints, for in the preliminary Chancery Court proceedings this unfortunate man had incurred the Lord Chancellor's censure. Bowes extended scant sympathy. 'I lament most exceedingly', he wrote, 'that I have been the involuntary cause of the troubles you have lately experienced and are still likely to sustain. However, I cannot conceive that you are thought culpable, except that it was from your being the entire author of preventing Lady Strathmore from gratifying her feelings when I think in regard to her eldest daughter an exertion of them might have been expected, and, I will venture to add, ought not to have been left short.'

The Lord Chancellor had ordered Bowes, Lady Strathmore and Lady Anna to return at once to England. It pleased Bowes to pretend that he, of course, would have gladly returned to face the music, but that Lady Strathmore would rather die than risk being parted from her daughter.

Having thus shifted the blame Bowes went on to make still further demands on his long-suffering friend. 'You have neglected me much by not keeping your promise of visiting me. I shall set out for Calais early tomorrow morning. By your meeting us, you will have an opportunity of stating matters in their true colours to both the ladies. As to myself, I am ready to attend the wishes of the Chancellor, and to confess I assisted Lady Strathmore in the execution of this affair.'

Having decided on Calais as their meeting-place, Bowes next day changed the *rendezvous* to Lille—'You will find me at the Hotel de Bourbon, sur la Grande Place.' Complete secrecy was to be maintained. Reynett was not to be told of the meeting.

Bowes did not go to Lille. Writing to his friend there on September 12th, he explained that he was confined to bed in Paris with a painful and violent rheumatic fever. 'But' he added, 'I am determined to quit this place tomorrow, and shall be with you as expeditiously as my disorder will permit. I do assure you I have felt extreme distress at the apprehension that you may have been waiting.'

This was cool enough in all conscience. Bowes must have known very well that the wretched Davies had been waiting for him at Lille; and a closer acquaintance with Bowes' illnesses suggests that the rheumatic fever was a mere excuse to avoid an interview which he dreaded. In the end Bowes left Paris and went to Lille, but only after he was quite sure that his friend would have tired of waiting and would have returned to England. On September 16th he writes from the Hotel de Bourbon, 'I have for some time suspected that Dame Fortune has forgotten her old connection, and left me upon the barren shore to shift for myself. But that suspicion is no longer one, it is realized by the mortification I have met in not finding you here'; and he then embarked on a rambling explanation about a letter which he had written to Davies at Lille asking him to stay for a few days more having been found by himself 'at the bottom of a drawer in the bar, along with yours of the 13th, neither of which would the sagacity of the people here have allowed me, had it not been for my own researches, after being repeatedly told there was no letter for me, and that they did not recollect any gentleman of your name being here'.

Davies must have had some hard thoughts about his friend, but Bowes' letter concluded, 'Your attendance at Calais, in case Mr. Scott should be in the least doubtful relative to Lady Strathmore's hopes, will be absolutely necessary; as soon as this letter is in the post, I shall set off for that place and shall get there on Tuesday evening.'

On September 19th Bowes wrote from Calais in a reproachful strain. 'I shall wait here till I see or hear from you, with that impatience which naturally arises from my situation and the perpetual agonies of distress that attends Lady Strathmore and her daughter from the dread of being parted from each other. . . . But your friend Strode told me that Newmarket could not do without you.'

The case came on in the Chancery Court; and Mr. Lee and Mr. Scott certainly did their best for their clients. Lady

Strathmore, they pleaded, had been the mover of the transaction from affection for her daughter; her ill health was due to her having been deprived of the comfort of her children; Bowes had acted the part of a benevolent husband by thus waiting upon her wishes. Both these 'high and humane characters', Foot states, 'pleaded with their eyes brimful of tears'.

The Lord Chancellor was unmoved by this display of emotion and ordered William Davies to proceed at once to Calais to bring Lady Anna back to England. The poor man had a very bad reception when he reached Dessein's hotel. Lady Strathmore was longing to leave France, which she detested; but this did not suit Bowes' books and for two days after his arrival he would not allow her to see Davies, claiming that her sensibility would be too greatly outraged. William Davies, and it would be difficult to blame him, was 'almost disposed to return the second time without her and Lady Anna and take all consequences with the Lord Chancellor'.

By the beginning of October the whole party was back at St. Paul's Walden, which they left almost at once on a visit to Buxton. At Buxton, Bowes' conduct was particularly outrageous, Lady Anna testifying that her step-father had burned her mother's face with a candle and had thrust a quill of a pen into her tongue. Lady Strathmore broke down and admitted to Mrs. Morgan that 'she wished God would take either her or Bowes so that her sufferings might end'. Mrs. Morgan was obliged to lay out £100 of her own money to provide her mistress with the clothes which Bowes denied her. Lady Strathmore, encouraged by Bowes, resorted to laudanum. After Christmas, Lady Anna returned to school in Queen Square; and in February Lady Strathmore exhibited Articles of Peace against her husband.

3

Before Lady Strathmore took this decisive step, she had escaped from her husband's house.

The Unhappy Countess

On January 24th, 1785, Mrs. Morgan, who had been dismissed by Bowes from Lady Strathmore's service, received a message from her late mistress by the hand of Ann Parkes, a housemaid, telling her that the countess feared that her life was in danger or at least that she was in peril of being confined for life by Bowes; and asking her to help her to escape. Mrs. Morgan, as she afterwards testified, believed that Lady Strathmore's fears were well founded, and she immediately enlisted the aid of a barrister cousin, a Mr. Shuter, who lived in Cursitor Street. Mr. Shuter agreed to make the necessary arrangements for Lady Strathmore's accommodation if she succeeded in making good her escape from Grosvenor Square. 'Bowes,' Mrs. Morgan later declared, 'was of a very cruel, savage and tormenting disposition . . . always unhappy himself and desirous of rendering all around him unhappy.'

On February 3rd, Bowes was to dine out in Percy Street, and Lady Strathmore, with the assistance of Ann Dixon, her housekeeper, Ann Parkes, the housemaid, and Thompson, her footman, laid her plans. The servants who were not in the conspiracy were got out of the way on some pretext. The chaplain, who had been detailed by Bowes to act as warder, was despatched to the stationer's to buy a book. Some doors were locked, and between six and seven o'clock in the evening Lady Strathmore, accompanied by Ann Dixon, left the house and reached Oxford Street undetected. Incidentally she left all her valuable jewellery behind— it was subsequently retrieved by the invaluable Mr. Davies. In Oxford Street there was a check, for there was no hackney coach on the stand. Eventually they got a coach and, just as they came opposite to Berners Street, they saw Bowes, also in a hackney coach, driving fast with his head out of the window. Fortunately he did not see them, but it had been a narrow escape and Lady Strathmore fell into hysterics. The two women reached Mr. Shuter's house in Cursitor Street, where they were joined by Mary Morgan and Ann Parkes. From Cursitor Street Lady Strathmore was taken to Dyer's Buildings, in Holborn, where rooms had been reserved for her in Mr. Watson's lodging house. Here, under the protection of a tipstaff appointed by the High Court, she was safe for the time being, though she took the precaution of going under the name of Mrs. Jefferies. Bowes quickly discovered her whereabouts, and took lodgings in the same street in order to keep an eye on her proceedings. But he did not dare to lay hands on her.

From her sanctuary in Dyer's Buildings Lady Strathmore took the three legal steps that were open to her. She exhibited Articles of Peace against Bowes, citing beatings, scratchings and other cruelties to her person. Next, being, as she correctly stated, completely destitute and without funds of any kind and possessing only the clothes she stood up in, she exhibited a Bill of Complaint against Bowes in the High Court of Chancery to have the Ante-Nuptial Indentures of January 9th and 10th established; to set aside the Deed of Revocation of May 1st as having been executed under duress; and to have a receiver appointed of the rents and profits of her estates, Bowes and his agents to be restrained from receiving the same. Finally she instituted a suit in the Consistory Court of the Bishop of London in order to obtain a divorce from Bowes on the grounds of cruelty and adultery.

The Articles of Peace were quickly disposed of in the King's Court Bench. Bowes was bound over for twelve months in his own security for a large sum and in the security of two friends, John Lee, the barrister, and the Duke of Norfolk.

Lady Strathmore's Bill of Complaint in the Chancery Court and her divorce suit in the Ecclesiastical Court were much more complicated.

The Court of Chancery, at this date, had only two Judges —the Lord Chancellor and the Master of the Rolls—and was still mediæval in pattern. In order to set its mechanism in motion, the plaintiff in an action had to begin by addressing a Bill to the Lord Chancellor by way of complaint against the defendant. This Bill of Complaint was an enormous document, setting out the plaintiff's case three times over, the third time in the form of interrogatories to the defendant.

The Unhappy Countess

The defendant was then served with a *sub poena* calling on him to answer the Complaint; but he was told nothing of the nature of the claim until he had appeared and had paid the officials of the Court for a copy of the Bill. The defendant could then put in his answer to the Bill, or reply to the interrogatories, or lodge an objection in law.

For proof of the case on either side, no witnesses were ever heard in Court. Elaborate interrogatories for the examination of witnesses were prepared by counsel, and upon these the witnesses were examined in private by officials of the Court, neither of the parties nor their lawyers being present. All the answers were put down in writing. Nothing in the way of cross-examination was allowed; and there was no verbatim record of what a witness had said. When all the evidence had been obtained in this way, the parties could get official copies of it.

It was to this cumbersome process that Lady Strathmore committed her fortunes. Bowes duly put in his answer to her Bill of Complaint, insisting on the validity of the Deed of Revocation of May 1st. This answer was known as the Cross Bill, or the Cross Suit.

On July 16th, 1785, the Court was moved on Lady Strathmore's behalf that it might be referred to one of the Masters of the Court to appoint a proper person to be receiver of the rents and profits from the Bowes estates; and that such a receiver might be directed in the first place to pay and discharge the interests on all mortgages, annuities and incumbrances, next to pay and allow to Lady Strathmore the sum of £1,500 towards her support and maintenance and towards her costs and expenses since the separation, and to make her a further allowance of a proper and sufficient sum for her support and maintenance.

At this point it would appear that Lady Strathmore's legal advisers were none too sure as to the outcome, for they advised their client to reach agreement with Bowes that all matters in dispute between them should be referred to arbitration; and Bowes agreed to this course of action. By November, however, Bowes had evidently plucked up

courage and had persuaded himself that he would win, for
he instructed his attorney to inform those acting for Lady
Strathmore that he would not consent to arbitration after all.
In Trinity Term, 1786, he exhibited his Cross Suit against
his wife, praying that the Deeds of 9th and 10th January
1777 should be declared null and void and be delivered up
to be cancelled on the grounds that they were fraudulent,
as having been executed by Lady Strathmore before marriage without his knowledge and in derogation of his rights
as a husband; that he should be given an account of the
rents and profits from the estates in dispute; and that he
should be decreed by the Court of Chancery to be well
entitled to those estates during the joint lives of himself and
Lady Strathmore. Lady Strathmore put in an answer to
Bowes' Cross Bill—and the battle was joined.

The procedure of the Ecclesiastical Courts was just as
cumbersome. All matrimonial jurisdiction, at this date, was
vested in the Church, and exercised in the first instance by
the Bishops' Courts; so it was in the Bishop of London's
Consistory Court that Lady Strathmore's citation against
Bowes was taken out. Her advisers had set down a com-
prehensive list of offences: beating, scratching, biting, pinch-
ing, whipping, kicking, imprisoning, insulting, provoking,
tormenting, mortifying, degrading, tyrannizing, cajoling,
deceiving, lying, starving, forcing, compelling, and wringing
of the heart; as well as a long record of Bowes' adultery and
illegitimate children. In answer, Bowes put Lady Strathmore's *Confessions* in the hands of the proctors, 'to make the
most of them'.

The Bishop's Court did not move very quickly. It was in
February, 1785, that the original citation was taken out.
Over the next thirteen months endless depositions were
taken, for here, too, the examination and cross-examination
of witnesses was conducted not orally and in open Court but
on paper by one of the Court's officers. Each side submitted
a list of questions which were put to the opposing party by
the Court's Examiner, and written objections could then be
taken to the answers given. It was not until all the evidence

had been given that the case was set down for hearing. The advocates for each party—the practitioners before these ecclesiastical courts belonged to a distinct branch of the legal profession, advocates and proctors approximating to counsel and solicitors—argued as to who was entitled to judgment on the record.

In Lady Strathmore's case, depositions were taken from surgeons and doctors, from successive chaplains and their wives, and from innumerable servants, male and female, employed or once employed in Grosvenor Square, at Gibside and at St. Paul's Walden.

In May, 1786, the Judge concluded the cause and assigned it for sentence and hearing. The case against Bowes was proved and he was ordered to pay his wife £300 a year alimony. But before sentence was confirmed, Bowes, in order to achieve delay, appealed to the Provincial Court of Canterbury, known as the Court of Arches, because it had originally sat under the arches of Bow Church. This right on the part of the defendant in a divorce suit to appeal to a higher Court was akin to the right of opting for trial by jury.

And so, when the twelve months of Bowes' binding over ended, the proceedings in the Chancery and in the Ecclesiastical Courts had both come to a temporary standstill.

Balancing the probable outcome of the suits, Bowes evidently concluded that the greater danger to his own prospects lay in the divorce proceedings. He therefore decided to take the law into his own hands and to put an end to that suit by summary methods of his own devising.

CHAPTER FIVE

The Abduction

Bowes' position, ever since his wife had escaped from his house, had not been an enviable one. As Foot put it, 'all the foul weather birds were hovering about his distressed house in Grosvenor Square; there used to come, one after the other, such a draggle-tailed set as are seen in wet weather canvassing about at elections'. He spent his time attempting to bribe witnesses and trying to think up some new scheme. He employed more than a dozen agents, none of whom knew what the others were about. One of the maidservants in the house was with child by him, and he hastily sent her away, lest the Doctors' Commons should get hold of her. He sat up all night drinking hard and eating high seasoned things, particularly peppered biscuits.

As soon as the twelve months of his binding over had ended and his two securities had been discharged, he began to formulate his crazy plan. If he could persuade or force Lady Strathmore to sign a paper agreeing to drop her divorce suit in the ecclesiastical courts or if he could, by fair means or foul, induce her to resume, or appear to resume, cohabitation with him, and thus prove condonation, then an end would be put to the divorce action, which he regarded as a greater danger to himself than her Bill of Complaint in the Chancery Court.

But Lady Strathmore had escaped from his clutches, and he had to move warily.

If Bowes' personal fortunes had deteriorated, things had begun to look up a little for Lady Strathmore who, at this time, was described as 'hopeful but very low'. Financed by her lawyer—for until and unless the Chancery action was decided in her favour she could not touch a penny of her income—she moved from Dyer's Buildings, first to a house in Hart Street and then to another larger and better house in Bloomsbury Square, where she once more had a coach at her command.

But both she and her advisers were, with good reason, apprehensive of her husband's intentions. While she was at Dyer's Buildings she had written a letter—which was never sent—to Lord Mansfield, the Lord Chief Justice, expressing the fear that Bowes might attempt to kidnap her and urging that any document she might sign under such circumstances should be regarded as invalid, as it would have been extorted from her under duress.

So Bowes' first move was to lull his victim into a false sense of security; and with this object in mind, at the end of September, he went north to Gibside, where he indulged in a farcical escapade, the sole evidence for which rests on an anonymous ballad, *Paddy's Progress, or the Exploits of an Irishman in England*. In all other respects this ballad is so well informed and is so clearly the work of a resident of County Durham who knew Bowes and his associates intimately, that it is hard to discount the extraordinary incident which it relates concerning Bowes' pretended suicide. And, to give Bowes credit, the best possible method of allaying Lady Strathmore's fears at this juncture would have been a rumour that he had died by his own hand.

A certain Dr. Brown had attended Lady Strathmore when she was in residence at Gibside, and early one Sunday morning a pitman, by the name of Chapman, presented himself at Dr. Brown's house in Newcastle and announced that Bowes had shot himself during the night in his dressing-room at Gibside. Hot on his heels came Joseph Hill, Bowes' groom, who begged the doctor, when he sent word to Lady Strathmore of what had happened, to intercede with her ladyship to allow him to remain on in her service. The next arrivals at the doctor's house were a party of Gibside pitmen. They had been told of Bowes' suicide and wanted to know who would now be responsible for paying their wages. Dr. Brown, who must have had his suspicions, refused to go to Gibside to inspect the corpse and referred all his callers 'to the attorney at the Quay'. Unwilling to incur the expense of a legal con-sultation, the pitmen returned to Gibside where they were greeted by a smiling Bowes, who enquired, 'Well, lads, did you really think I was dead?'

Whatever Bowes' intentions had been, this crazy idea had misfired and was explained away as a joke; and in the second week of October Bowes came south, bringing with him a friend by the name of Peacock, later described as 'a respect-able coal merchant of Newcastle upon Tyne'; Chapman, the pitman who had broken the news to Dr. Brown and who generally went under the name of Cummins; and another pitman called Pigg. These two, as the leading counsel for the Crown was subsequently to observe, 'were people that were accustomed to dark deeds by living in a mine'.

From this point onwards the story is well authenticated by innumerable depositions.

Bowes travelled to London by by-roads; called himself Colonel Medison (or Maddison, or Medecin, or Morrison—witnesses were splendidly various in their rendering of this alias); wore a large bush wig; and at Stone in Staffordshire engaged a post-boy, Peter Orme, who in due course was to prove a valuable witness for the Crown. Orme was engaged at a wage of £20 a year and a guinea down.

Arrived in London, Bowes established his gang in a house he had leased, No. 18, Norfolk Street, from which vantage point he kept a careful watch on his wife's movements. He invariably went out armed and in disguise—for a time as a Justice of the Peace in a big long-tailed wig and spectacles, and later 'in a sailor's dress with trowsers'. This last deception was to astonish the Crown Prosecutor. 'How the Devil (for no-one but the Devil could devise such schemes as these), I say how the Devil could put in his head to think of a sailor he must explain to you; a most remarkable disguise for such a project, and more peculiarly so as the object of his persecu-tion was a woman—creatures of all others most beloved by British tars.'

The Unhappy Countess

Be that as it may, 'Colonel Medison' and his friends haunted Bloomsbury Square, both on foot and in hackney coaches with the blinds up; and Lady Strathmore soon became aware of his activities and confided her fears to Mr. Mingay, a barrister who had already appeared in Court on her behalf.

Some move on Mr. Mingay's part must have alarmed Bowes, for he decided that another attempt must be made to quiet his wife's suspicions; and so, leaving Peacock, Chapman and Pigg in Norfolk Street, he took the road north with his French valet, Prevot, arriving at Streatlam Castle on October 21st, where he was welcomed by Henry Bourne, the Streatlam steward, who was prepared to go to any lengths that Bowes might suggest.

The Gibside doctor, Dr. Brown, had been a disappointment. It was now decided to try out Mr. Hobson, a surgeon who practised near Barnard Castle. Mr. Hobson was summoned to Streatlam Castle, Bowes asked him if he could keep a secret, and having explained that circumstances made it necessary that he should go into hiding, a plan was agreed on. Next day Bowes made a public appearance at the Barnard Castle cattle market.

The accommodating Mr. Hobson, who believed that Bowes wished to hide from his creditors, played his part well. Riding back from the market Bowes, Prevot and Bourne passed a Mr. Thomas Colpitts, who knew them all well by sight. After they had been gone a sufficient time to have got to the Castle and further, Colpitts saw Bourne riding back. The steward stopped at Mr. Hobson's house, summoned the surgeon, and then went to the post-house where he announced that his master had had a bad fall from his horse. Colpitts, arriving later at the scene of the accident, found Bowes lying near the turnpike, attended by the surgeon and apparently dead. His head was resting on a pile of stones and there was a little hay under him. They had just blooded him, Colpitts was told, and the surgeon reported that his patient had broken three ribs, that blood was coming out of his ears, and that he thought his shoulder was out. At this point Bourne came back with a post chaise and took the money out of his master's pocket—'£1,400, I heard them gingle the money into their hands' as Colpitts reported. Bowes was carried off to Streatlam Castle, news of the accident was printed in the papers, and the numerous enquirers were told that the invalid was making slow progress but would be too unwell to receive visitors for a very long time.

Mr. Hobson, as the Prosecution was to suggest, 'must have been one of the most astonishing surgeons in the world', for on October 28th his bedridden patient was back on the road to London; and as soon as he reached Norfolk Street Bowes caused a search to be made for lodgings behind Bloomsbury Square in order to be nearer his victim who, as he fondly imagined, supposed him to be lying seriously ill at Streatlam.

The search for lodgings brought Bowes' gang into touch with a Mr. Edward Crook, who kept the Pyed Bull in Russell Street. Mr. Crook was suspicious of Chapman, Pigg and Prevot—'upon my word, I took them for a gang of thieves. I would have nothing to do with them'—but a visit to 'the Justice', Colonel Medison in person, sitting in a great armchair and wearing his great wig with the long tail, convinced the inn keeper of the truth of their story that they had come five or six hundred miles in pursuit of robbers; and he volunteered that he knew a constable who might be of assistance to them, one Edward Lucas, popularly known as 'Four Eyes'.

The bespectacled Lucas, formerly a corn chandler in High Holborn and more lately head runner to Mr. Justice Walker, proved to be just the man they needed; and in return for lavish promises he called on Lady Strathmore in his official constabular capacity, informing her that he had seen some suspicious looking fellows lurking round her house and offering her his protection. This offer was gratefully accepted, Lucas was taken on the strength at a wage of twelve shillings a week, and escorted the countess whenever she left her house.

The stage was now set, and on November 8th Chapman went to the office of Mr. Justice Walker, Lucas's former employer, and made oath that he went in danger of his life from Mrs. Morgan, Crundell and Jones—respectively body servant, coachman and footman to Lady Strathmore. A warrant was duly granted and was handed to Lucas, who obtained the services of three other constables to do a part of his dirty work for him.

On the morning of November 10th, the day which Bowes had chosen, Lucas went as usual to Lady Strathmore and asked if she was going out. She paid him what was due and told him that she was driving out between one and two in the afternoon, but that she would not require him to accompany her on this occasion as a friend, Captain Henry Farrer, brother to her solicitor, had promised to escort her.

That afternoon, when Lady Strathmore's coach drew up outside Mr. Forster's ironmongery shop in Oxford Street, one of the suborned constables who, with Lucas, Prevot, Peacock, Chapman and Pigg had been following in a couple of hackney coaches, at once arrested Lady Strathmore's footman and coachman, hauling them off before Mr. Justice Walker. Terrified, Lady Strathmore, Mrs. Morgan and Captain Farrer hurried into Mr. Forster's shop and locked themselves into an upstairs room where they waited until there was a knock on the door.

'Who's there?' Lady Strathmore called.

'Your friend Lucas.'

'Ah, Lucas! Open the door.'

As soon as Lucas entered the room he seized his employer's arm, pulled out his constable's staff and exclaimed, 'My God, my lady, you are my prisoner. I have a warrant against you. I must carry you to Lord Mansfield at Caen Wood. It is as much as my life is worth not to execute it.'

Mrs. Morgan indignantly demanded, 'Can you seize a countess as you can a common person?' to which Lucas retorted that there was a warrant out against her, too, and that she had better make her escape. Mrs. Morgan took herself off, going straight to the office of Farrer and Lacey, Lady Strathmore's solicitors. Lady Strathmore, accompanied by Captain Farrer and Lucas, got back into her coach, now manned by Bowes' confederates, and was driven off as she supposed to Caen Wood, by way of Tottenham Court turnpike and Highgate.

At Highgate a halt was called at the Red Lion inn where, in an upper room, they were joined by Bowes. Lady Strathmore threw up the window and shouted murder.

Still under the impression that she was being taken to Caen Wood, Lady Strathmore was induced to re-enter her coach, dragging Captain Farrer after her 'step by step'. Bowes was now with them in the coach and they were closely followed by a hackney coach containing two of the suborned constables with Chapman and Pigg. When Lady Strathmore protested that they were not going in the direction of Caen Wood, and when Captain Farrer supported her, Bowes threatened to throw the captain out of the window. Lady Strathmore was clinging to her friend's arm and Bowes said, 'Damn you, madam, are you not ashamed of yourself when your daughter lies dying?' Shortly afterwards, he politely requested Captain Farrer to leave the carriage, adding that if he did not do so he would knock him down. Captain Farrer said he was a gentleman and would have satisfaction for such an expression; but he meekly left the coach and had to walk back to London.

Lady Strathmore was carried on to Barnet where, at the Adam and Eve in the Barnet Road, Peter Orme, the postboy, who had been waiting with a hired chaise since 11 a.m., joined the cortège. Lady Strathmore, by this time, had succeeded in breaking the glass in the coach window and was crying murder again. To anyone curious enough to ask what was going on, Bowes explained that his wife was mentally deranged.

At the Red Lion at Barnet fresh horses were put in; and on arriving at the Bell at Stilton, at one o'clock in the morning of Saturday, November 11th, Lady Strathmore was taken into a room where Bowes called for pen, ink and paper and, having written a few lines and holding a pistol at her head, demanded his wife's signature. She refused, saying, 'I will not sign it for you or anybody.' Whereupon Bowes threw down his pistol and struck her a blow with his clenched fist.

When they left Stilton, Lady Strathmore had to be forced into the coach by Chapman and Peacock and, as they drove along, Peter Orme saw Bowes beat his wife on the face and body. When she cried out, he thrust a handkerchief into her mouth and on the most trifling contradiction struck her with the chain and seals of his watch.

By noon—they had travelled right through the night—they reached the Angel at Doncaster. The carriage stopped in the street and fresh horses, which had been ordered ahead, were immediately put in. At Barnby Moor, Lady Strathmore was shown into a room, attended by a chambermaid, and Bowes was all impatience, standing at the bottom of the stairs and calling several times to hasten her down. At Ferry Bridge she had to leave the coach 'to go into the garden'. Bowes waited at the door. At midnight they reached Streatlam Castle where they were received by Bourne, the steward, and by a servant, Mary Gowland, who was suspected of being Bowes' mistress. On the steps, Lady Strathmore cried out that she was brought there by force and desired that it might be made public. Bowes tried to bribe the postilion who had driven them on the last stage from Greta Bridge to say that the carriage had nearly upset and that it had been this that had frightened Lady Strathmore.

Tired as she must have been—they had driven from London in thirty-three hours—Lady Strathmore was subjected to further badgerings and threats. In the dining-room Bowes confronted her once more with the document he had drawn up at Stilton and when she again refused to sign this renunciation of her divorce suit he held a pistol to her head, bidding her say her prayers as he was going to kill her. She told Bowes to fire. 'By God,' he exclaimed, 'you are an astonishing woman.'

Chapman and Pigg, who with Prevot, Lucas and Peacock had followed their master up the Great North Road in a hackney coach, then carried Lady Strathmore up to bed—'two Abigails,' as it was observed at the trial, 'that she had not been used to before.'

The Abduction

Worse, far worse, was to follow; but already Lady Strathmore's friends were moving on her behalf.

James Farrer, Lady Strathmore's solicitor, was in Carlisle, but Mrs. Morgan and Captain Farrer had told their story to his partner, Mr. Lacey, and Mr. Lacey had gone straight to Lord Mansfield, the Lord Chief Justice. Lord Mansfield sent one of his tipstaffs, Ridgeway, to Streatlam Castle with a writ of Habeas Corpus and a 'Rule for Information against the persons concerned in seizing and carrying off by force the Right Honourable the Countess Dowager of Strathmore', a document which expressed the hope that 'all Persons would give their Assistance in having her Ladyship produced to the Court of King's Bench'.

In the meantime, the news that Lady Strathmore was being held a prisoner in the Castle had quickly spread round the neighbourhood, and pitmen from the surrounding Strathmore collieries, organized by John Langstaff, one of the colliery managers, gathered in considerable force in the park. Fires were lighted, and they shouted that they would rescue the countess, alive or dead.

Late on Sunday evening, November 12th, Thomas Bowes of Darlington, Stoney Bowes' solicitor, arrived at the Castle in response to a summons from his client. The doors had been bolted, no lights were permitted, and the windows were all shuttered, but this privileged visitor was allowed into the fortress. Next day, at about 3 p.m., Ridgeway, the tipstaff, reached Streatlam from London but was unable to gain admittance. When he called out, a gentleman whom he took to be Stoney Bowes—but who was, in fact, Thomas Bowes, the lawyer—came to the door and on him Ridgeway tried to serve the writ of Habeas Corpus and the Rule of Information. Thomas Bowes indignantly refused to accept service, slammed the door in Ridgeway's face, and then spoke to the tipstaff through a window. Ridgeway, calling out 'Take notice, I have served Andrew Robinson Bowes by putting a copy of the Habeas Corpus under the door, and I deem it good service,' then pushed the documents under the front door, where they were later found by Peter Orme, the post boy.

The Unhappy Countess

Ridgeway returned to London to tell the Court of what he had done.

On Wednesday, Mr. James Farrer, who had been informed by express letter of what was afoot, arrived at Streatlam from Carlisle, was denied admittance, and went away. Next day he returned and this time was allowed in by Thomas Bowes 'on parole', for the purpose of 'conversing with him and with no-one else'. But by this time Lady Strathmore was no longer in the house. Having searched the Castle for her, James Farrer left, telling Thomas Bowes that he would not be in his skin for the County of Durham.

Between 11 p.m. and midnight on the Monday night Bowes had come into his wife's room with a great coat belonging to Thomas Bowes and a servant's bonnet in his hand and had told her she must dress and come away with him. Mounted pillion behind Chapman, Lady Strathmore had been taken to a cottage nearby occupied by Mary Gowland's father, and here she had been shut up 'in a dark press where the bed was'. Bowes had threatened her with a visit from a 'mad doctor' and a strait waistcoat.

Lady Strathmore remained in Gowland's cottage until around midnight on Thursday, November 16th, when Bowes, his unwilling wife, Mary Gowland, Chapman, Pigg and Matthew Shields, a gamekeeper in Bowes' employ, embarked on a flight that was as fantastic as it was apparently purposeless. Bowes had taken fright because his pursuers were closing in on Streatlam.

In wintry weather and in the pitch dark, with snow lying on the high ground, they drove over Bowes Moor, arriving at between 5 and 6 a.m. at Matthew Shields' cottage at Argill, where Lady Strathmore was forced to go to bed in a room with two beds in it, the second bed being occupied by two of the menservants. Later she had to dine in the kitchen with the gamekeeper's family; and at 3 o'clock that afternoon the party, complete with Matthew Shields, set off again. At 6 p.m. they stopped at the house of David Kirk, turnpike keeper at Brough Corner. All the men of the party, Kirk was to declare, were armed. Bowes carried Lady Strathmore into

The Abduction

the house. She was wet, cold and distressed and had lost one shoe and a stocking. Bowes explained that his wife had a daughter who was lying-in and that she was on her way to visit her. Lady Strathmore was allowed to stay by the fire for a quarter of an hour before the party moved on again in the direction of Appleby. The weather, Kirk later testified, was extremely wet and stormy.

At 8 p.m. they reached James Aungier's inn at Appleby, where they supped and went to bed. Next morning, November 18th, they set out in two post chaises for Penrith—it was hinted at the trial that Bowes intended to ship Lady Strathmore over to Ireland. Three miles out of Appleby, on the Penrith road, Bowes was told by an ostler that pursuers in a post chaise were less than a mile behind him. He leapt out of the chaise; and Lady Strathmore was unwillingly hauled out after him and was mounted pillion behind Chapman on one of the chaise horses. The post-boy was told to drive his post chaise on to Penrith in order to deceive the pursuers.

That afternoon Bowes, now calling himself Dr. Hopper, a mad doctor, arrived at Brampton and, explaining that his chaise had broken down, asked for a horse to take him to Coupland Beck, where another chaise would meet him. From Coupland Beck the party went to the house of one John Lamb, at Esplan Moor, and thence, guided by Lamb, along a range of hills to Burton, where they called at a cottage. Lady Strathmore, starved and desperately cold, shed tears and was seen to wring her hands. 'Dr. Hopper' explained that she was out of her mind. At the cottage, Mary Gowland treated her very roughly. From Burton, with Lady Strathmore still riding pillion behind Chapman, they returned to Matthew Shields' house at Argill. The weather was stormy, with snow lying in places to a depth of three to four feet. On one occasion the horses stuck fast and Lady Strathmore had to be carried over the snow. She tried hard to speak to Lamb, who was still with the party, but was prevented. She did manage to say to him, 'Tell them I'm here. Tell them I'm here.' She was frozen and very distressed.

At 4 a.m. on the morning of Sunday, November 19th, Lady

117

The Unhappy Countess

Strathmore was brought to Thomas Bowes' house in Darlington. A maid in the house was woken by Mrs. Bowes, who
demanded a light. The girl was then forbidden by her mistress to leave her room or to get up. She was not allowed out
of her bedroom as long as Lady Strathmore was in the house.
The windows of the room occupied by Lady Strathmore
were kept shuttered.

On Sunday afternoon Lady Strathmore was forced into a
chaise again and driven by way of Durham to Newcastle,
arriving at the Queen's Head that evening. Bowes immediately ordered four fresh horses to take them to Choller-
ford, on the Carlisle road. By this time it was dark, stormy,
and raining hard. The glass in the window of the chaise
broke, and at Harlow Hill a halt was called. The horses were
taken out and the draughty chaise, with Lady Strathmore
and Mary Gowland inside it, was wheeled into a stackyard
where pigs were kept. The chaise and its occupants remained in the yard from 10.30 p.m. till 3 next morning.
Bowes then ordered the post boys who had driven them from
Newcastle to drive to Morpeth, but the boys refused because
of the darkness and the bad weather, more especially as
Bowes wished to reach Morpeth by side roads.

Bowes had apparently been expecting some friends to join
him at Harlow Hill, and their failure to arrive made him
irresolute and confused. Eventually he ordered the post boys
to drive them back to Newcastle, where he wandered from
place to place, visited Mr. Peacock's house, drove out on the
Shields road and then turned back, and finally gave the two
post boys a guinea apiece and told them to keep his return to
Newcastle a secret.

But by this time the alarm had been given and the country
had been alerted.

On November 20th James Farrer had announced a
Reward of Fifty Pounds in these terms:

'The Court of King's Bench has granted an Attachment
against Andrew Robinson Bowes Esq., for forcibly taking
away the COUNTESS OF STRATHMORE, and Mr. Ridgeway, his
Lordship's tipstaff, and others, are in pursuit of him to

execute such Attachment. Any Person concealing or secreting the said Countess of Strathmore, or aiding, abetting, or assisting the said Andrew Robinson Bowes in taking the said Countess of Strathmore from place to place to elude Justice, shall be Prosecuted with the utmost Rigor and Severity of the Law.

'Whoever shall bring the said Countess of Strathmore to James Farrer, Esq., now at Carlisle, shall receive a Reward of FIFTY POUNDS from that gentleman. The like Reward will be paid by Mr. Farrer on bringing the said Andrew Robinson Bowes Esq., and his armed ruffians, to him at the City of Carlisle aforesaid.

'N.B. An Express is arrived from Newcastle mentioning that Bowes and his Ruffians, with Lady Strathmore, set off from that Town yesterday, and are supposed to be going to Port Patrick, and from there to Ireland.'

On November 21st, James Farrer issued this description of 'Lady Strathmore, Mr. Bowes and his Ruffians':

'Mr. Bowes is above the middle size, sallow complexion, large Nose which stands rather one side, and lisps in his speech.

'Lady Strathmore is a little woman, a longish Face, with fine dark brown Hair, rather Bulky over the Chest—Mr. Bowes gives out that she is Dumb, and sometimes Disordered in her Mind—Her Ladyship does not speak.

'Edward Lucas, one of Mr. Bowes' Ruffians, is a Middle Aged Man, looks quick, an acquiline Nose, a striped second Mourning Coat, and a light coloured Great Coat, a light two or three Curled Wig, in general wears spectacles.

'Francis Peacock, a very tall and stout Man, above six feet four inches high, dark Complexion, a little pitted with Small-pox. Lucas and Peacock were yesterday at Carlisle, lurking about and looking for Intelligence.'

After her adventure was over, Lady Strathmore carefully pasted these posters into her album. At the bottom of one of them the following postscript is added in handwriting:

'Since the above, it is supposed that Mr. Bowes and Lady Strathmore are in the neighbourhood of Brampton—

despatches have been sent to every part of the Kingdom to stop the progress of the greatest Monster that ever disgraced Society. It is presumed they only travel by night—poor Lady Strathmore had but one slipper without stockings when they arrived at Brough, from whence they went into the Bishoprick of Durham, Newcastle etc.. The Country will no doubt endeavour to Release a valuable Woman from her present deplorable and distressing situation by searching every suspected Place and pursuing them till taken.'

With the countryside thus alerted, Bowes, with Lady Strathmore and Mary Gowland, drove out of Newcastle on the Durham road, Marc Prevot riding behind them. They were now being pursued by one Abraham Dunn, who had been hired by Lady Strathmore's aunt, Mrs. Liddell, to prevent Bowes getting fresh horses at the inns. Half way between Durham and Darlington Dunn saw Bowes priming two pistols; and at this point Bowes promised the postilions five guineas apiece to take him as far as Darlington with the Newcastle horses. At Aycliff, five miles short of Darlington, Robert Thornton recognized the occupants of the chaise and joined in the pursuit. Bourne the steward then caught up with the party and warned his master how close his pursuers were. Bowes had Lady Strathmore out of the chaise, mounted her behind him on a blanket, and took to the fields.

At midday Dunn and Thornton called upon Christopher Smith, constable in the parish of Neasham, to arrest the fugitives; and Smith and several other Neasham inhabitants set off in pursuit of the riders.

Christopher Smith described his part in the story in an affidavit:

'An alarm was given by a man on horseback that Bowes had killed his wife and the country was in arms to take him. I had seen a man ride past with a woman behind him, without a pillion, attended by another man on horseback, wanting a hat or any covering on his head, and a bare sword by his side, and took them for pickpockets. Upon this, I ran to the door and said to my brother, "Let us each get a stick, and we will go and take him." We went after them, as did several of the village, about a mile into Sockburn Lane. Upon our coming up, Mr. Bowes said, "What do you want?" I said, "The country is alarmed with a bad report, we are come to take you." Mr. Bowes presented a pistol and said he would blow out the first man's brains that dared touch him. I said, if he would surrender, we would not hurt him. He again said he would shoot anyone that came nigh him, and that he would pay anyone who would take him to Northallerton. John Gunston said the Tees was too deep at Sockburn, he must go back to Neasham. I said he should not stir from the place till he was taken, and if he would not submit we would set upon him, and take him at all events; for he was a suspicious person, and had surely done something bad, or he need not ride through the country in the manner he did.

'Mr. Bowes turned about his horse, seeming to go away, when the woman slipped off from behind him and, clasping her hands together, said, "I am Lady Strathmore, for God's sake assist me." I said, "Are you indeed Lady Strathmore?" She said, "I am, and am forced away contrary to every inclination by that man (pointing to Bowes)." I said, "If you are Lady Strathmore, we will secure your person, and take him"; and bade the men get sticks and we would set upon him, and take him at all events.

'Anthony Claxton put off his hat, and went near Bowes, which, I perceiving, told him to put on his hat and be upon his guard; and seeing Bowes rest the pistol upon the other I rushed upon him and seized them both, and called for assistance, when John Wainton came and took hold of the horse and led him past me. While Bowes struggled with me, one of the pistol handles broke in my hand, and by pulling them away, the guard of the trigger cut a piece out of the foremost finger of my right hand. I threw that pistol away, and with the other gave Bowes a blow upon the right side of his head which knocked him from his horse.

'Fearing he had more pistols about him, and that he might shoot some of us, I gave him another blow upon the back part of his head, and cut it about two inches. Lady Strathmore asked if he was killed, and desired we would not strike him

The Unhappy Countess

again, and several times bade us search his pockets for pistols and take care he did not shoot some of us. Her Ladyship, being then on upon horse before Gabriel Thornton, bade us farewell.

'I sent John Gunston away for the surgeon to dress the wound, and took him to Eliza Shutt's till Thomas Bowes, Mr. Turner, and Mr. Rudd's man came and dressed the wound, and then carried Bowes away to Thomas Bowes' house in Darlington. And on the Wednesday he was conducted to London by three men.'

Marc Prevot made off, and it was some considerable time before he and Edward Lucas were rounded up. Both, incidently, fell on evil days and Bowes never raised a finger to help them.

Lady Strathmore wasted neither time nor sympathy on her husband. She left at once for London in the company of two of her gallant rescuers—Christopher Smith's account of the incident is a refreshing glimpse of rustic courage in support of law and order—and eventually reached Mr. James Farrer's house in Bread Hill Street late on the evening of Tuesday, November 21st. Here she retired to bed completely prostrated. Next morning she was examined by a surgeon, Mr. Beaumont, who reported that she was in such a desperate state from exposure, exhaustion and cruel treatment that he considered her life to be in considerable danger. She was unable to stand or to walk unsupported for a month.

CHAPTER SIX

Bowes at Bay

On November 23rd, 1786, two days after she had returned to London, Lady Strathmore once again swore Articles of Peace against her husband, this time citing instances of cruelty to her person on the journey north to Streatlam; during her term of imprisonment in the Castle; and in the course of her subsequent wanderings.

Four days later Bowes, escorted by officers of the Court, reached Barnet, from which place he despatched a note to Jesse Foot informing the surgeon that he would shortly be arriving in London and would require his professional services. He followed up this letter in person, driving not to Foot's house, as he said he would, but to Atkinson's Hotel in Dean Street. Foot went straight round to see him. He found his patient as pale as ashes, with a week-old beard, his head bound up with a bloody handkerchief, his boots dirty, and his shirt and cravat stained with blood. Foot gave him some mulled wine, but 'his stomach rejected it'.

The officers of the Court required their prisoner to proceed straight to Westminster Hall. Bowes tried to persuade Foot to go in his place and to explain that he was too ill to attend. Foot refused to take this responsibility without the support of a second medical opinion. A Dr. Kennedy was called in, who said he thought that Bowes could safely attend. On the way down to Westminster, Bowes was sick twice; and as he passed through the Hall, leaning heavily on Foot's arm, he was greeted with hisses.

The legality of the service of the writ of Habeas Corpus and of the Rule of Information having been proved, Bowes' counsel pleaded that his client should not be committed to prison, as there was no accommodation there for a man in his delicate state of health. At this, the Marshal of the King's Bench prison observed in a loud voice, and amid considerable laughter, that he 'could accommodate the gentleman'. So Bowes was driven to St. George's Fields where the Marshal rented the 'state rooms' in his own house to his wealthy prisoner. And in the King's Bench prison, or within its rules, Bowes was to stay for the twenty-two remaining years of his life.

Foot visited him frequently, reporting that for the first three weeks after his admission Bowes was 'taken up with those adjustments which are found necessary for all who seek for comfort in such abodes of accommodation'. His wounds healed satisfactorily; but Foot was disgusted to learn that the sickness and pallor of his patient on the day of his arrival in London had been caused by a dose of ipecacuanha, Bowes having bought this drug in Barnet and having swallowed it as soon as he had reached Atkinson's Hotel. 'This was done', Foot writes, 'in order that his appearance might excite commiseration and to avoid, if possible, being committed to prison.'

In the matter of the Articles of Peace sworn against him by Lady Strathmore, Bowes was bound over to keep the peace for a term of fourteen years, in his own security of £10,000, and in two securities of £5,000 each. Through his counsel, he protested strongly against the length of the term and the amount of the bail.

In prison, Bowes soon perked up; became reconciled to the Marshal's 'state rooms'; and had his plate brought in so that he could entertain.

His trial on a charge of abducting Lady Strathmore was hanging over his head; but in the meantime he still had the spending of his wife's income and the control of her estates. In order to further his cause, he purchased an interest in a newspaper, *The Universal Register*, and between November, 1786, and April, 1787, a long and tedious correspondence appeared in the pages of this Journal. The letters, signed

'Justus', 'Truth', and 'Vindex', in turn attacked (rather mildly) and defended (with considerable spirit) Bowes' past conduct and current activities. All these letters were written by Bowes himself—a hero fighting with his own shadow.

In May, when he had been in prison for five months, and while the Crown was still collecting evidence, Bowes' counsel, the Hon. Thomas Erskine, successfully applied to the Court of King's Bench for a reduction in the length of the term of his client's binding over and in the amount of the bail. Mr. Justice Ashurst reduced the term to two years, though he observed that the defendant stood charged 'with as daring an outrage as ever was committed in a civilized country'.

Flushed with this success, and in order to avenge himself on 'his' county Durham tenants who had openly sympathized with Lady Strathmore, he advertised twenty-four tillage and stock farms on the Streatlam Castle estate to let. He set out the names of the sitting tenants in the advertisement, which closed with this ominous warning: '*N.B.* To save trouble, and to encourage new tenants, it may not be improper to add that NONE of the above people will be treated with upon any terms.'

He also embarked on a bitter attack on James Farrer in the columns of *The Universal Register*, accusing the lawyer of harbouring Lady Strathmore for sinister purposes of his own. And on May 29th, on the eve of his trial, he printed the following paragraph in his newspaper:

'It is said that a certain society of married gentlemen, in the neighbourhood of St. James's, in case Mr. B. succeeds in defeating the strange machinations of his amiable lady, propose a subscription in honour of his meritorious services to the enemies of *petticoat government*, and the friends of matrimonial subordination.

'It is thought that the subscription will be much larger than that which was made to give a statue to Mr. Howard; as the taming of bad wives is a matter of infinitely greater importance to society than a casual improvement of the policy of a prison.'

The Unhappy Countess

On May 30th, 1787, Bowes and his fellow conspirators came up for trial in the Court of King's Bench before Mr. Justice Buller and a Special Jury on a number of charges; among them, conspiring to take and imprison Lady Strathmore in order to oblige her to drop a prosecution then depending in the Ecclesiastical Courts by which she sought to obtain a divorce from Andrew Robinson Bowes; conspiring to imprison her; and assaulting and imprisoning her without stating a conspiracy.

Mr. Mingay, Mr. Law and Mr. Garrow appeared for the Crown; the Hon. Thomas Erskine, Mr. Chambre and Mr. Fielding for the defendants.

After Mr. Mingay had told the full story of the abduction, embellishing its recital with a wealth of irony, Mr. Erskine did his best for his clients. He pointed out that an indictment for perjury against Lady Strathmore, sworn by Bowes, stood next for trial, in the course of which many of the countess' statements, relied upon by the prosecution, might well be proved false. On the most serious of the charges, that of conspiring to stop the prosecution of Lady Strathmore's divorce suit, only Bowes, he emphasized, could be guilty, because only he had been aware of his real purpose in carrying his wife off. There was, he admitted, no defence in law for Bowes having illegally taken his wife into his possession, but there were strong mitigating circumstances. A husband might take into his own possession a wife who wantonly lavished away the property of her husband. Furthermore, it was legal to remove a wife out of the hands of people who wished to make a breach between them wider, 'more especially when, to effect so diabolical a purpose, witchcraft and fortune-telling is used'. These conditions had obtained in Bowes' case, and therefore Bowes had behaved laudably. 'I wish in the execution of that pursuit,' Mr. Erskine admitted, 'he had acted with caution. From the evidence laid before you he certainly has not. I cannot justify him, but I hope to mitigate his crime.' He suggested that the Jury should find that all the defendants except Bourne and Thomas Bowes had conspired to imprison Lady

Strathmore, but that they had not conspired to stop the suit in the Spiritual Courts, for they had known nothing of it. As regards Thomas Bowes, Mr. Erskine declared that he had acted solely as Stoney Bowes' attorney; that he had not known that Stoney Bowes had had the intention of carrying off Lady Strathmore; nor had he aided and abetted him in that intention. The same arguments applied to Bourne, the Streatlam Castle steward.

His efforts on this occasion were in vain. The jury, having listened to the case from nine o'clock in the morning until half-past four in the afternoon, brought in their verdict without retiring and after only a few minutes' consideration. All guilty of the whole charge. The Judge announced that sentence would be pronounced at a later date.

Bowes' indictment of Lady Strathmore for perjury stood next for trial, but Mr. Erskine explained that his client had been consulting him upon the propriety of trying this unfortunate lady; and not to further wound her feelings, he had advised him not to prosecute the indictment now before the Court. The jury therefore found her not guilty.

Twenty-seven days elapsed between conviction and sentence, and Bowes made use of the interval to publish the following advertisement in *The Universal Register*:

'Preparing for the Press and shortly will be published, AN ACCOUNT of the life of M. E. Bowes, including a Narrative of her Conduct from the age of 13 till a short time previous to her elopement from her present husband. Written by herself.'

It is perhaps easier to forgive Bowes for his physical cruelties than it is to pardon him for offering Lady Strathmore's *Confessions* to the public, more especially as he prefaced the printed version with a verse of his own composition:

> When hoary age the lustful passions bend,
> Compunctions oft the matron's bosom rend;
> Then comes CONFESSION, eager to disclose,
> The *Source* and *Cause* of all her present woes.

The Unhappy Countess

On June 26th, Bowes, Lucas, Peacock, Prevot and Bourne were brought up in custody of the Marshal of the King's Bench prison in order to receive sentence. The case against Thomas Bowes was not proceeded with.

Once again Mr. Erskine pleaded in mitigation of Bowes' conduct. The idea behind the 'abduction', he explained, had been to withdraw Lady Strathmore from a conspiracy 'that had been practised on both their happiness'. 'If,' he said, 'I could have proved that after they had gone two stages from London she was perfectly reconciled; if I could have proved that she embraced Bowes as her deliverer; it would not have altered the verdict, because undoubtedly Bowes acted illegally.' But the time had come, Mr. Erskine declared, to explain Bowes' real motive. Very reluctantly, his client had decided to strip off his wife's mask in order to explain his own conduct. So the story of the Ante-Nuptial deeds was re-told; and a great deal was made of the 'elopement', which was described as a conspiracy on the part of Mrs. Morgan, George Walker and the housemaid, 'who kept Lady Strathmore as a lunatic confined, and who made a prey of her'.

Mr. Justice Ashurst was unimpressed by these arguments and, in passing sentence, observed: 'The crime . . . of which you have been found guilty, does appear to be of as atrocious and daring a nature as ever appeared in a Court of Justice, and had not the facts been made out by the most incontestable proofs, one would hardly have thought that in a civilized country, governed by such laws, any set of men would have been found hardy enough to take away a lady of rank and fortune from one of the most public streets of this great town, at midday, in defiance of all law, order and government, and to drag her through the heart of the Kingdom 240 miles; and what is a high aggravation of the offence is, that it was meant and intended to impede the current of public justice; and by force and violence to put a stop to a prosecution legally instituted by her against you, for cruelty and adultery.'

Bowes was fined £300 and sentenced to three years' imprisonment in the King's Bench prison, 'at the expiration of the said term to find securities for fourteen years, himself in £10,000 and two securities of £5,000 each'. Lucas was fined £50 and sentenced to three years' imprisonment in Newgate. Peacock was fined £100 and sentenced to two years in the King's Bench. Prevot was given one year in Newgate; and Bourne was fined £50 and sentenced to six months in the same prison.

Bowes moved into what were described as 'inferior state rooms'; but he was still paying rent for accommodation in the Marshal's quarters, outside the actual prison itself; and he was evidently able to make himself pretty comfortable, for his household included Mr. and Mrs. Peacock, their daughter, master William Johnstone Bowes and 'requisite servants', Mary Gowland among them.

For the next twelve months, he busied himself with a restless tangle of schemes and plans and consultations with his lawyers. The abduction trial was behind him. That was something over and done with. The three years' sentence of imprisonment would soon pass. What really mattered to him were the pending suits in the Chancery and in the Ecclesiastical Courts. If they went in his favour, then he would come out of the King's Bench prison a rich man. If they went against him, he would be irretrievably ruined.

But his mind occasionally strayed from these legal issues. On July 13th he despatched Jesse Foot to Lant Street, in search of the daughter of a fellow prisoner who was in the King's Bench for debt. The charms of this girl had caught his eye when she had paid her father a visit in prison. Foot found Jenny Sutton 'a girl of perfect symmetry, fair, lively and innocent. She was feeding a pigeon with split peas out of her mouth.'

In due course Jenny Sutton joined Bowes in his apartments. He hired a room for her on the same staircase; she never appeared when he had company; she was most jealously guarded; and she remained with Bowes until he died. 'She was blessed', Foot writes, 'with a native cheerful disposition and found a channel for her affections in her children. She had ever been a child of misfortune; all which particulars marked, adapted and qualified her for being a true and rare representation OF A FEMALE OF FORTITUDE.'

Bowes' behaviour in prison would seem to have been no less unpleasant than his behaviour when he had been at large. He had always been fond of practical jokes, and one of his favourite tricks when he had people to dine with him in the Marshal's apartments was to urge his guests to help themselves to the spirits that were on the table, while he himself filled up their glasses with water from a silver tea kettle. As the kettle, on his instructions, had been filled half with water and half with spirits, the more anxious his guests were to remain sober, the drunker they were likely to become. This amused him very much. It is horrifying to think that the silver kettle he employed for the purposes of this squalid deception may well have been the beautiful kettle by Simon Pantin which his father-in-law, George Bowes, had commissioned in 1724.

Bowes was still in control of Lady Strathmore's estates; and was determined to allow no one to forget it. On October 1st he circulated the following letter, discreetly headed 'St. George's Fields'.

'No person has any right to receive the Streatlam Estate rents except the receiver or receivers appointed by the Court of Chancery under the claims of a mortgage for the sum of £6,500 raised by the late Earl of Strathmore and that when the transfer of the mortgage is made (as it will be soon) then THE RENTS OF THE ESTATE WILL REVERT TO ME or Mr. H. Bourne. Lady Strathmore NEVER CAN OR WILL possess any power over, or any right to receive the rents of the said estate during THE TERM OF MY LIFE. I will only give her an allowance or alimony unless she quits the society of artful, interested attornies and menial servants . . . or unless some respectable persons among her relations or former friends will take her under their charge and protection.

'No debts incurred by Lady Strathmore or Mrs. Morgan, since Lady Strathmore's elopement, will be paid by me or, according to my firm belief, by any other person whatever.'

The fact that James Farrer was financing Lady Strathmore evidently annoyed Bowes intensely; and in January, 1788, he addressed an open letter to his wife's lawyer which was published in the *Newcastle Chronicle:*

'You then came boldly forward, the active knight-errant of a distressed matron, and, with the spirit of a Quixote, vauntingly threw down your gauntlet as the champion of immaculate innocence against what you declare to be the brutal designs of a savage husband.' Lady Strathmore, he went on, had been the worst of wives to Lord Strathmore, who had died of a broken heart. When she had eloped from his house, she had 'deserted three of her children by three different husbands'; and by offers to servants she had attempted to bring about his own assassination. Mrs. Morgan was described as 'the absolute governess of Lady Strathmore's person and understanding. Does she not dictate the whole of her conduct with all the imperious impertinence of an upstart tyranny? And you abet her.'

After her return from the north, Lady Strathmore had remained for weeks on end in her bedroom at Mr. Farrer's house in Bread Hill Street. Her relations seem to have been happy to allow the lawyer not only to give her sanctuary but also to advance her very considerable sums of money. But Lady Maria and her brothers George and Thomas all came at one time or another to see their mother. On December 28th, 1786, the *London Packet* printed the following letter:

'Lady Strathmore returns her sincere and hearty thanks to her friends . . . for their humane and spirited exertions towards the restoration of her liberty, and the preservation of her life. . . . She is able to inform her friends that she is at length in a fair way to recovery from the painful and alarming effects of her late sufferings, and gains strength daily.'

She also wrote to thank John Langstaff for his exertions in organizing the rally of pitmen in Streatlam Park:

'Lady Strathmore returns her very sincere and particular thanks to Mr. Langstaff for his most judicious and active exertions in her favour, which she must always remember with heart-felt gratitude.

The Unhappy Countess

'Lady Strathmore has the pleasure to add that she is greatly recovered within these last three days, having regained the use of her limbs in what at first seemed to threaten a mortification, so far as to walk the floor with a stick.'

On the last day of December she came downstairs for the first time and dined with the Farrers; and in January a house was taken for her in Holles Street, into which she moved with the faithful Mrs. Morgan. In March she was indicted for perjury by Bowes in connection with her evidence in the abduction trial, James Farrer and Mr. Forster, the Oxford Street ironmonger, standing bail for her. As we have seen, this charge was eventually dropped. In May she followed the abduction trial with intense interest; and it is perhaps significant that she pasted into her press-cuttings album, with comments in her own handwriting, every single newspaper account of the trial, every scurrilous ballad, every pamphlet, notice or document with any bearing on the case that she could lay her hands on. Even cuttings from newspapers published in India were represented. It is difficult to avoid the conclusion that she still liked, rather than disliked, publicity; and that she was, in truth, a very good hater.

2

On March 8th, 1788, some ten months after Bowes and his fellow conspirators had come up for trial in the abduction case, the Lord Chancellor, sitting in Lincoln's Inn Hall, heard the two depending Chancery Causes—the Bill of Complaint filed by Lady Strathmore praying the Court to substantiate the deeds of January 9th and 10th, 1777, which had vested her life interest in her father's estate in the hands of trustees; and the Cross Bill, filed by Bowes, stating that these deeds were fraudulent, and praying that they might be set aside and that the Deed of Revocation of May 1st, 1777, under which the control of his wife's life interest had passed to himself, might be established.

The Attorney-General, Mr. Partridge and Mr. Richards appeared for Bowes, and presented his case. The deeds of

January 9th and 10th, they claimed, were fraudulent and should be set aside since Bowes had married in ignorance of their existence. The case must be considered as it stood at the time of Bowes' marriage to Lady Strathmore, or immediately afterwards. The Court could take no notice of anything that had passed since then. 'This Court will not hold any act valid that was done by either man or woman, in disparagement of the rights to be acquired by the other by marriage.' The argument put forward by Lady Strathmore's counsel that the deeds were not fraudulent because they were executed not with a view to her marriage with Bowes but with a view to her marriage with Grey would not do. 'Can a widow be permitted to make such a provision, defeating the marital rights of a second husband?' One of the rights a husband acquired by marriage was to take the profits of estates of which the wife was in possession. The wife could not, by private conveyance, deprive him of those rights; and in this instance no provision was made, under the deeds, for the children of the first marriage. Again, if the deeds were set aside, was Lady Strathmore entitled to have a provision made for her by her husband? Bowes' counsel argued that she was not so entitled, because she had been guilty of fraud. Therefore Bowes must be put in the same state as if she had never executed the deeds. Lady Strathmore could not, in law, put herself in a better position than she was in.

The Lord Chancellor ordered that the parties should proceed to a trial at law on the following issue: whether the Deed of Revocation of May 1st, 1777, had, or had not, been obtained under duress.

This was a perfectly usual procedure, for if a case involving common law arose in the course of a Chancery action, the Lord Chancellor would require it to be heard and considered either in the Court of King's Bench or in the Court of Common Pleas. As Blackstone put it: 'If any matter of fact is strongly controverted, the Court [The High Court of Chancery] is so sensible of the deficiency of the trial by written deposition that it . . . usually directs the matter to be tried by jury.'

The Unhappy Countess

Whether Bowes had or had not obtained Lady Strathmore's signature to the Deed of Revocation by duress was a strongly controverted matter of fact; and the Lord Chancellor, before he could proceed further with the case, required it to be decided one way or other by a jury.

The issue was duly tried at Westminster Hall before Lord Rosslyn, Lord Chief Justice of the Court of Common Pleas, and a special jury. The jury found that the Deed of Revocation had, in fact, been obtained by duress.

This decision, a damaging blow to Bowes' case, was reported back to the Court of Chancery; and on June 19th, 1788, the two Causes—Lady Strathmore's Bill of Complaint and Bowes' Cross Bill—came up for a further hearing, Mr. Justice Buller sitting for the Lord Chancellor, with Master Holford and Master Ord. In his judgment, Mr. Justice Buller made the following points:

He agreed with Bowes' counsel that Bowes could not be considered as standing in Grey's place, or as bound by what Grey had been bound by. There was no proof, indeed, that Bowes knew what Grey would have been bound by. As he saw it, the 'dry question of law' embraced two sets of cases: the first relating to women who had never married and had no children; the second to women with children by a first husband. In the first category, fraud consisted in falsely holding out that an estate was unfettered and that the husband would of course be entitled to it. In the second class it would certainly be fraudulent if the wife held out that there was no settlement, even if the settlement was in favour of a child by a previous marriage. But no case had ever established a rule that all conveyances by a wife were void merely because the husband had not been told about them. It had to be proved that the husband had been *deceived*, mere concealment alone was not enough. Further, in *Rex v. Cotton*, it had been stated that there was no fraud or imposition on a husband who did not pretend that *he* could make a settlement. Mr. Bowes sought equity. He must therefore do equity. He demanded that the Deeds of January 9th and 10th should be set aside, without himself offering to make any provision for his wife. This, the Judge declared, was a ground for refusing relief to the husband. In all cases where a husband came to the Court for his wife's fortune, he must make a settlement. As late as January 16th, 1777, Lady Strathmore had intended to marry Grey. The story of a sham duel had been stated in evidence and had not been contradicted. A man who began by such a strategy was not entitled to consideration in a Court of Law. A man who married without a marriage treaty must be content to take the wife as he found her.

Bowes' Cross Bill was dismissed with costs, Bowes being ordered to pay his wife her costs as taxed at law in the original cause. The Deed of May 1st, 1777 (the Deed of Revocation) was to be surrendered to Lady Strathmore and cancelled. The Deeds of January 9th and 10th, 1777, were to be established. Bowes was to give up to his wife all plate, jewelry, and other possessions that were in his hands. 'The said George Stephens (the survivor of the two original trustees) being alleged to be abroad', a receiver was to be appointed to administer Lady Strathmore's estates.

Bowes, as was his right, petitioned the Lord Chancellor that the two causes should be re-heard. And re-heard they were, on March 3rd, 1789, before the Lord Chancellor.

On this occasion it was Mr. Richards who, on Bowes' behalf, propounded the doctrine of a husband's rights.

A wife, he argued, by marriage contract, became extinct for several civil purposes, with regard to which she merged with her husband. He became liable for all her debts, and answerable for all her acts that did not amount to felony— and even for felony, if committed in his presence, because her mind was supposed to be in his coercion. In order to enable him to undertake these responsibilities, he had, by the law, all her property; and it was absurd to say that the wife should be able, by her own act, to deprive the husband of what the law had given him. As for Bowes having made no settlement, in this case it could not have been necessary, for Lady Strathmore had had a very large income, a great estate for her life, and much personal property.

The Unhappy Countess

He produced another material proposition. Marriage, by the law of England, gave the husband the whole dominion over the property, and also over the person, of his wife, except as to murder, for by the old law he could not be punished for cruelty to her. He was head of the family: to make another would be against the policy of the law. If the wife could, by her own act, and against the consent of the husband, make herself independent of him, it would destroy the subordination so necessary in families. If Lady Strathmore was right in what she had done, the husband had become a cypher in his own house, for he could not educate his children or do any other act which by law he had a right to do.

Mr. Mansfield, Mr. Harding, Mr. Law and Mr. King appeared for Lady Strathmore. A want of communication, they argued, was something very different from concealment. Bowes could have no part or lot in this property for it was not in Lady Strathmore at the time of her marriage, having been previously vested in trustees. It was a settlement made by a woman for the protection of her children. Bowes had made no settlement on the Countess, though he had some fortune from a former wife. He took Lady Strathmore as she then was, with what she then had, therefore there was no fraud. Knowing that she was a woman subject to sudden and violent impulses of generosity, he had made use of a vile artifice to obtain her by means of a sham duel ('for it is at every stage of the case admitted to have been so') and he then forced her into the revocation—a thing he would not have done had he not thought the original deed a good one. Bowes had not been cheated; and to make the Ante-Nuptial trust valid was only to put a safeguard in Lady Strathmore's hands against the consequences of an impoverished marriage.

The Lord Chancellor, in delivering judgment, observed that he never had a doubt about this case. A conveyance by a wife, whatever the circumstances, and even at the moment before marriage, was *prima facie* good, and became bad only upon the imputation of fraud. As to the morality of the transaction, he would say nothing as to that. The parties seemed to have been pretty well matched. Marriage in general seemed to have been Lady Strathmore's object; she was disposed to marry anybody, but not to part with her fortune. The settlement of January 9th and 10th, 1777, was to be considered as the effect of a lucid interval, and, if there could be reason in madness, by doing this she had discovered a spark of understanding. Even if there had been a fraud against Grey, he could not have allowed Bowes to come to the Court and complain of it. But there had been no fraud, even against Grey. It was impossible for a man, marrying as Bowes did, to come into equity and talk of fraud; therefore the decrees of January 9th and 10th must be confirmed with costs.

The Lord Chancellor's decrees were signed and invoked on April 6th, 1789. It was referred to a Master in Chancery to take an account of the rents and profits received by Bowes from his wife's estates since the commencement of the suit. On June 9th, 1791, the Master reported that the sums owing by Bowes amounted to £10,295 11s. 1d. On October 19th, 1796, Bowes appealed, unsuccessfully, to the House of Lords; and in the course of this appeal it was stated that from 1788 he had been in contempt of the Court of Chancery for not paying to Lady Strathmore her taxed costs for trying the issue at law; for not delivering up the deed of May 1st, 1777; and for not giving back family plate, jewels, etc. From 1791 he had been in contempt for not paying further taxed costs and the £10,295 11s. 1d.

3

It will be recalled that in November, 1786, when Lady Strathmore was carried off to Streatlam Castle, her divorce suit was awaiting the hearing of Bowes' appeal to the Court of Arches.

On November 30th, 1786, a few days after his return to London under arrest, Bowes had had the impudence to give in to the Court an 'allegation of mutual forgiveness', on the grounds that he had cohabited with his wife from November 12th to November 20th—'the days,' as Mr. Mingay was to observe during the abduction trial, 'of her misery and persecution . . . the days previous to those in which she appeared to be frozen to death—he pleaded they had lived for eight days in mutual co-habitation and forgiveness— Co-habitation on the mountains in snow!'

Had this allegation of mutual cohabitation and forgiveness been upheld, it would have brought the suit to an end, as condonation has always been, and for that matter still is, an absolute bar to relief. But the Court of Arches did not uphold it, the Judge pronouncing against Bowes' appeal. Bowes was ordered to pay the taxed costs amounting to £1,742 14s. 2d. and to pay his wife the sum of £300 a year for alimony.

But he had one more card to play. The final right of appeal in matrimonial cases had originally been to Rome. This had been abolished by Henry VIII, and had been replaced by an appeal to the High Court of Delegates. And to the High Court of Delegates Bowes appealed.

On February 13th, 1789, the Lords Commissioners heard the cause of divorce brought by Lady Strathmore against her husband.

Bowes was charged separately with cruelty and with adultery; and on the subject of cruelty Lady Strathmore's counsel, Dr. Bever, made some illuminating generalizations in his opening speech. 'The cruelty,' he observed, 'must be such by which the peace and happiness of the wife is entirely destroyed, by which her person is perpetually attacked and terrified, by which her rest and comfort are destroyed, and she is deprived of that kind of happiness and of those enjoyments which, by the Matrimonial Contract and by every law, both human and divine, she is certainly entitled to. My Lords,' he went on, 'this kind of conduct is capable of very great exaggeration and will alter its complexion and will on many occasions become much blacker and will also on many occasions become more and more atrocious, it will become more and more so in accordance to the Education, the Fortune, the Rank and the Condition of the Person both of him who inflicts and of her who suffers it. My Lords, the case now before your Lordships is not upon the common wranglings and disputes between John and Betty, that kind of beating can do no worse, perhaps, than break a head without wounding a heart, and does not consist in anything more than broken heads and bloody noses which are the common consequences of the marriage state and which are very easily and very happily made up by a little matrimonial consolation at night—that is not the cruelty we complain of.'

The social standing of the parties having been satisfactorily defined, the whole sorry story of pinchings, burnings, beatings, restraints and petty tyrannies was gone over once again, and was contested and argued every inch of the way by Bowes' counsel, Dr. Battie, who had this to say for his client:

'I conceive I may venture to declare that her [Lady Strathmore's] conduct was such it would make every species of rigour not going absolutely to acts of cruelty but, however, every species of coercion and restraint, not only justifiable in Mr. Bowes, but, in my opinion, absolutely necessary. I mean it justifies him if I can show, and I flatter myself that I can, from the answers given to several of the interrogatories, that her conduct was such as to raise strong suspicions in Mr. Bowes to justify great rigour and severity . . . I mean to say this is a great excuse for a husband who behaves with some degree of rigour and severity to a wife under such circumstances. I do not know how I should feel upon it, but I fancy any man that had a wife and knew she was criminal with the Footman would behave with some degree of severity.'

The reference to Lady Strathmore's alleged misconduct with her footman, George Walker, was a pointer to the line of Bowes' defence, which took the form of attacking his wife's character and conduct.

Lady Strathmore, it was claimed, had been 'extravagant, lustful, wicked and abandoned in temper and disposition';

and 'in the indulgence and gratification of her lusts and other profligate means' she had contracted large debts before her marriage. She had behaved to her husband with 'the utmost insolent contempt and disobedience and with the greatest impropriety and indecency'. She had had criminal intercourse and connection with George Grey and, having entered into a contract of marriage with him, she had been threatened with an action for recovery of damages, to settle which £12,000 had been paid. Bowes had only treated her with 'the strict attention' and 'had laid such restraints on her conduct' as she had appeared to want and as had seemed good to him after reading the *Confessions* of her past life. On his marriage she had been found to be pregnant. She had always had a handsome and proper wardrobe; he had been rendered uneasy when her appetite had failed; and her decline in health had been due not to his cruelty but because she had been deprived of the company of her children. She had had criminal intercourse with the footman, George Walker, whom he had dismissed from his service but who had been taken back by Lady Strathmore into her employment; and with Thompson, a gardener at Gibside.

In support of Bowes' case against his wife were the depositions of a number of his old friends and employees. Eliza Stephens had deposed that Lady Strathmore was a woman without any sense of religion or morality, much addicted to the gratification of her lusts, drinking frequently to excess until she became intoxicated and so little able to take care of herself that she had more than once set her clothes on fire. She had spoken of Lord Strathmore's death as 'a release' and had said she loved cats better than her children. Bowes had at all times been very proper and indulgent in his behaviour to her and had betrayed a great degree of persuasiveness. She confirmed the story of Lady Strathmore's relations with George Grey and dilated at length on the countess's improper partiality for George Walker.

The Rev. Henry Stephens, who by this time had become Curate (in the absence of a resident vicar) of Ponteland in

Northumberland, described Lady Strathmore as 'dissipated and extravagant to an unbounded degree . . . violent and sudden in her attachments . . . without regard to the principles of religion, decency or morality'. As he had observed it, the conduct of Bowes towards his wife had been invariably kind and indulgent; and Bowes had been a thoughtful and affectionate step-father. He was convinced that Lady Strathmore had committed misconduct on innumerable occasions with George Walker.

The only witness whom Bowes could produce to testify to his wife's alleged misconduct with Thompson, the gardener, was Joseph Hill, his head groom at Gibside who, it may be remembered, was one of the principals in the farce connected with the pretended suicide.

Lady Strathmore's case against her husband, and her defence against his allegations, depended on the depositions of Mrs. Morgan, of the Rev. Samuel Markham and his wife, of Mrs. Frederick (a friend of the family), and of such of the past and present servants as took her side. She was, they deposed, 'a lady of a most meek, mild, obliging, tractable, humane and obedient temper and disposition'. During the time she and Bowes lived together she had constantly behaved to him with the greatest tenderness, affection and duty. Bowes had treated her with diabolical cruelty; had denied her society; had refused her money with which to buy clothes; had instructed the servants to ignore her orders; and had rendered her life miserable by his disreputable and adulterous conduct.

Evidence of Lady Strathmore's misconduct before her second marriage was not admitted by the Court—Bowes had submitted her *Confessions* to Doctors' Commons in vain; and his allegations that she had had criminal intercourse with Walker and Thompson were found to rest on very flimsy evidence. A faint doubt must attach to her relations with the footman. Certainly she had been indiscreet in admitting him to her confidence. Both she and Eliza Planta were said to have given Walker snippets of their hair; and there was a record of other gifts. There had been talk of her giving him a farm and later Walker and his wife were established at Great Ham in Northumberland. But on balance it seems likely that she was innocent of a charge which rested on the evidence of her spiteful and avowed enemies, Mr. and Mrs. Stephens.

On the other hand there could be no doubts about Bowes' cruelty and about his scandalous relations with women. On the score of his adultery, Lady Strathmore's counsel cited the cases of Mrs. Houghton, the wet nurse; Dorothy Stevenson, the under nurse; and the little maidservant, Elizabeth Waite.

Bowes' defence to these well attested charges was to dispute the facts; to answer, as we have seen, by recriminations against his wife's moral behaviour; and to claim that Elizabeth Waite had been a common prostitute, that his chaplain, Mr. Reynett, had been the father of Dorothy Stevenson's child, and that Mrs. Houghton's child had been by her own husband.

On March 2nd, 1789, the day before the Lord Chancellor gave judgment in the High Court of Chancery, the Lords Commissioners, assembled at Serjeants' Inn Hall, having heard the arguments of counsel and having consulted for half an hour, pronounced that 'Andrew Robinson Bowes, being unmindful of his conjugal vows, and not having the fear of God before his eyes, did, on the several days and times mentioned in the pleadings of this case, commit the several acts of cruelty therein mentioned, and did also on the days therein set forth commit the heinous crime of adultery. The Court therefore order and decree, that the said Andrew Robinson Bowes and Lady Strathmore be divorced, and live separately from each other; but that neither of the parties marry during the natural life of the other of them.'

'Thus,' as *The Gentleman's Magazine* noted, 'Lady Strathmore was at length restored to the large possessions of her family, and divorced from a marriage contracted in an evil hour, and which was a source of a series of bitter calamity to herself, but productive of a plentiful *harvest* to the *lawyers*.'

Bowes never paid a penny of the £300 a year alimony

ordered by the Court; and he failed to pay the taxed costs allowed to Lady Strathmore for prosecuting her suit in the Ecclesiastical Courts. These costs amounted to £1,742 14*s*. 2*d*. In 1790 he was duly excommunicated by the Judge Delegates for refusing to submit to the justice of ecclesiastical censure, and was thereafter charged by the temporal Court of King's Bench with writs of *excommunicado capiendo*.

4

Between 1787 and 1790, while the tide of the law was slowly restoring Lady Strathmore's fortunes and destroying Bowes', the two parties to the dispute, she in her house in Fludyer Street and he in the King's Bench prison, each lived the kind of life one could have predicted.

In October, 1788, a paragraph relating to Bowes' conduct in prison appeared in the *Morning Post*: 'To some people— but we do not allude to *debtors*—to some people a commitment to Banco Regis is no great punishment. A certain delinquent daily eats, drinks, and gets merry, and though surrounded by as many wives and children as MACHEATH, keeps them all in good order. . . . Among the evils that arise from imprisonment for debt may be reckoned the increase in female incontinence—the young women who attend on their unfortunate confined relatives being generally seduced. A recent instance of this kind has taken place, wherein poverty having expelled every generous feeling from the parent, he permitted the prostitution of his child to supply his wants, and she now lives openly with a prisoner of a different description. . . .'

In this same month of October, 1788, Bowes was pleased to champion the cause of Mary Farrer, the wife of Captain Henry Farrer who had been Lady Strathmore's companion on the occasion of the fatal shopping expedition in Oxford Street.

Bowes' motives were transparently clear. He had a deep grudge against James Farrer, Henry Farrer's brother; and in

The Unhappy Countess

his wife's friendship with the not very gallant captain he saw a chance of smearing her with a little more mud.

Henry Farrer's marriage, which had taken place in 1781, had been kept a secret from the rest of the Farrer family. It can be presumed that his wife belonged to a social class a little lower than that into which he might have been expected to marry. Nor had their life together been a happy one. If the evidence that Bowes collected and printed in a book—*The Appeal of an Injured Wife against a Cruel Husband, written by Mrs. Farrer and dedicated to the Countess of Strathmore*—is to be believed, Captain Farrer had proved a most unsatisfactory husband. He had failed from the start to provide his wife with a home or with sufficient funds, so that she had been obliged to work as a milliner and mantua maker and, when this occupation had proved unremunerative, she had had to offer her services as a cleaner of silk stockings and a clear-starcher of muslin and gauze. Worse, her husband had formed a connection with a Mrs. Parks; and later (in Mrs. Farrer's, or rather in Bowes', words—for he is believed to have been the author of the book) 'he carried on an intrigue of a still more nefarious and degrading nature—that he was connected with a married woman and for purposes the most wicked. The personage I refer to is the Right Honourable the Countess of Strathmore.' Mrs. Farrer (or Bowes) was very bitter about this friendship. 'The Captain now had two ladies to attend, and one of them a Countess—in such a situation he could not but consider that household-plague a wife except as an impediment to his pleasure and a drawback to his interest.' She accused her husband of attempting to seduce her sister (who put up a prolonged fight for her virtue); complained that Lady Strathmore frequently visited the captain in his chambers in the Temple ('a place where few modest women venture to visit'); and declared that she was 'convinced that notwithstanding Captain Farrer's regard for Mrs. Parks he would never have parted from me if it had not been for Lady Strathmore. By the one he was duped—by the other he was fascinated. . . . After Captain Farrer became *Protector* to Lady Strathmore, I

144

ANDREW ROBINSON BOWES

STREATLAM CASTLE

can safely say that my state was that of *widowhood*; for in no respect whatever did Captain Farrer conduct himself to me as a husband.'

Bowes did his best for the injured and deserted lady. After writing and publishing her life story he arranged a benefit performance in which she took the leading part. At his instigation, the following advertisement appeared in the *World* of December 2nd, 1788: 'The Lord Chamberlain has granted a licence for the performance of *Tamerlaine* at the Haymarket Theatre this present evening, in which Mrs. *Farrer*, who a short time ago published a pamphlet dedicated to Lady *Strathmore*, will perform the part of *Arpasia*, and there are flattering expectations that from her person, voice and expressive countenance she may prove a successful candidate for the winter theatres.'

Tamerlaine the Great, or the Fall of Bajazat, Emperor of the Turks, together with a farce entitled *Who's the Dupe?* was duly performed, the following note appearing on the programme: 'The Public are respectfully informed that the utmost care and attention will be taken to render the performance respectable and to merit their appreciation and support.'

Bowes took Mrs. Farrer into his apartments in the King's Bench and encouraged her in an action against her husband, which was settled out of court.

The pronouncement of the divorce, followed the next day by the Lord Chancellor's decree in the Chancery action, were fatal blows to Bowes' fortunes—indeed March 2nd and March 3rd, 1789, must have been the blackest days of his life. He had lost both his expensive battles; and if he wished to escape from prison he had to find some very large sums of money.

He either could not, or would not, pay these debts; and as Foot wrote: 'Thus mauled, stripped, disgraced and blasted, the prison bolts flew open, all of a sudden he bade adieu to the outer state rooms, and entered into the walls, in a pickle not unmerited, and in a state which, to some, death would have been comparatively an ELYSIUM.'

But Bowes possessed remarkable powers of recuperation. 'Like a tree struck by lightning, he had still a few green branches left. He had the best rooms within the walls and, as birds do when they are reconciled to the cage, he began to plume himself, to pick and meditate upon the possible smiles the place could afford him. He took an analysis of the inhabitants; and particularly all those he could make useful to his purpose he tempted by his dinners.'

He had quarrelled with Peacock; but he had Jenny Sutton with him and a growing family of illegitimate children. True to his nature, he made the best of a bad situation.

Lady Strathmore's life during these momentous years was uneventful save for one extraordinary incident. Lady Anna, her younger daughter, came to live with her in Fludyer Street. In December, 1787, her eldest son, John Strathmore, returned from Caen, where he was studying the French language; and after pasting a newspaper cutting giving this intelligence into her album, his mother added a rather pathetic postscript—'my son did come over for ten days, just to see me'. As soon as her divorce had been decreed and after the Lord Chancellor had restored her fortunes, the Lyon family seem to have decided once more to recognize her existence; and even Foot's Palace Yard friend resumed his visits.

But the one extraordinary incident that marked this period of gradual social rehabilitation is splendidly in character.

Understandably, Lady Strathmore's unfortunate experiences had given her a horror of the married state; and this was reflected in her treatment of Lady Anna, whom she virtually imprisoned in the house in Fludyer Street, refusing to allow her to go to parties or to make any friends with the opposite sex. Lady Anna did not take this treatment lying down. Denied ordinary social intercourse, she struck up an acquaintance with a young lawyer of the name of Jessup who lived in the house opposite. According to Anthony Morris Storer, who recounted the story in a letter to Lord Auckland, 'she had never seen this man but at his window'. But somehow love had blossomed, and one night, when everyone else had gone to bed, Lady Anna pushed a ladder which had a plank laid on it through her bedroom window and, Fludyer Street being very narrow, her lover, stretching out of *his* window, caught hold of it, and the intrepid young lady was able to cross over this unsubstantial bridge. 'Leander,' as Mr. Storer observed, 'was a Fool to her.' They ran off together; they were married; and the marriage turned out badly. Mr. Jessup died young, leaving Lady Anna with two daughters, only one of whom grew up to become, as readers of Augustus Hare's *The Story of My Life* will recall, 'Cousin Susan Davidson, of Ridley Hall'. As a widow, Lady Anna Maria Jessup—who, most confusingly, became known as Lady Maria Jessup—lived for many years as a pensioner of her brother at Bird Hill House, on the edge of the park at Gibside.

CHAPTER SEVEN

The Last Years of Lady Strathmore and Bowes

By no possible standards could Lady Strathmore have been described as a good mother; and it is ironical that from the year 1790 until her death ten years later her children should have been the main preoccupation of her life—though the innumerable small dogs which she kept ran them a close second.

In 1790 her eldest son, John, 10th Earl of Strathmore, came of age; and this was made the occasion for a general financial re-settlement. Lady Strathmore revoked the 'uses and trusts' of the famous Ante-Nuptial Indenture of January 9th and 10th, 1777, and declared new and other uses of the revenues and profits of her estates for the benefit of her eldest son and in order to make some provision for her two youngest children—Mary Bowes and William Johnstone Bowes. At the same time, John Strathmore, who had come into his father's fortune, purchased his mother's life interest in the Gibside and Streatlam Castle properties.

In this same year Lady Strathmore regained the custody of her two youngest children. A rather touching letter from Mary Bowes to her mother is preserved in the Bowes Museum.

NEWINGTON,
SURREY.

. . . I cannot express the joy it was to me to be informed by my Lady Wright of my turn of Fortune in being now, I hope, under your Protection. When I parted from you, I was much too young to know the loss of a mother. I am sensible of the duty and affection I owe to you and my Brother. . . . I long very much to see you and hope there is nothing more now wanting to complete my happiness. I am sure you will be very glad to see my dear little brother William, indeed he is a very fine Boy. Although I have been almost five years absent from you I have not forgot any place where I spent my infancy and believe I could find my way over one half of Paul's Walden and Gibside houses etc.

Pray assure the Earl of Strathmore of my grateful love, my dear Mama,

Your dutiful and affectionate daughter,

MARY.

The hand of John Strathmore can be seen in this knitting-up of a disrupted family. He was endlessly kind to all his brothers and sisters, including his half-brother and half-sister; and having disliked and neglected her eldest son in his youth, Lady Strathmore became devoted to him after he had grown up. Her album is stuffed with newspaper cuttings relating to his various social and political activities. A later hand has defaced most of the references to the friendship of this most attractive young man with the beautiful Lady Tyrconnel. His mother had had no such compunctions.

In 1792 George Bowes, the second son, came of age and his mother made over St. Paul's Walden to him, herself buying Purbrook Park, two miles from Cosham on the Portsmouth road. It was from Purbrook that she wrote a dignified letter to *The True Briton* and to the *Hampshire Chronicle* protesting against Bowes' re-publication of her *Confessions*. Her life in Hampshire was uneventful. In 1877, a very old farmer in the district recollected that she lived with two of her daughters, her maid-companion, Mrs. Morgan, and a full establishment of servants. 'She kept little company,' he recalled, 'and was much occupied with pets, especially dogs, of which she had many. Each one had its own bed in a basket, with everything to make it comfortable. Meat was regularly provided in the room which they occupied. Every day a hot dinner was cooked on purpose for them and

The Unhappy Countess

each dog had its own place set apart for him, with a plate and a dish.'

In 1796 the faithful Mrs. Morgan died. She was buried at Christchurch, and Lady Strathmore erected an elaborate monument to her memory, herself composing the inscription:

'DEDICATED to the most rare of all connections, a perfect and disinterested friend, by the Countess of Strathmore, who, conscious of the treasure, valued its possession and mourned its loss. . . . To her heroic qualities, her cool deliberate courage, and her matchless persevering friendship, the tears of blood shed by one who despises weakness, the records of law and justice, and perhaps even the historic page, will bear witness to an astonished and admiring posterity.'

The album continued to receive press-cuttings referring to Bowes' activities—his behaviour in prison and his renewed lawsuits—but the handwriting of the comments grew progressively shakier. In 1799 an alarming occurrence connected with William Johnstone Bowes produced a most satisfactory crop of newspaper stories.

William Bowes had joined the Royal Navy, and in February, 1799, was serving aboard the frigate *Proserpine*, Captain Wallis, bound for Cuxhaven, with Mr. Greville and despatches on board. The frigate, having run into packed ice in the estuary of the Elbe, had to be abandoned, and the crew and passengers walked eight miles over the ice to Newark Island. Twelve men, a boy, a woman and a child perished of cold. After staying on Newark Island for some days, William Bowes, with a few other officers and seamen, unknown to the Captain and without his permission, returned to the *Proserpine* and went aboard her. That night a violent storm got up, the ice shifted, and *Proserpine*, as the Captain wrote in his report, 'was swept to destruction; and with it, as I am miserably afraid, went the above officers and men'. But not at all. 'The ice', Captain Wallis later reported, 'supported the ship without quitting her, until after some days the wreck was cast on shore on the Island of

150

Baltrum, from which, providentially, they all made their escape.'

William Bowes was spared, only to lose his life in the disaster of the *Blenheim* in 1817. His half-sister, Mary Bowes, never married, and lived in Bath.

Lady Strathmore died on April 28th, 1800, and on May 10th was buried in her wedding dress in the South Cross of Westminster Abbey.

2

If the last years of Lady Strathmore's life were comparatively calm, Bowes', right to the very end, were hectic, turbulent and characteristically disgraceful.

He had one dominating passion—to regain control over at least a part of Lady Strathmore's fortune; and as solicitor succeeded solicitor, he hatched scheme after scheme to that end. In the meantime, life in prison was not without excitement and interest.

In the month of October, 1790, a fellow prisoner in the King's Bench, Mr. Vardy, went with £80 in his pocket to the apartment of Dr. Hodson 'who kept a hazard table in the same prison'. Bowes was present, and after a time Vardy discovered that most of his bank bills were missing. He reported their loss to Bowes, who threatened to throw him out of the window, seized hold of him, swung him backwards and forwards in the air, and then informed the unfortunate man that *he* had the bills—and dared him to take any remedy to regain them. Vardy sued Bowes, who was fined 6*s*. 8*d*., the Marshal being informed by the Judge that it was his duty to suppress gaming in the prison. In the following April John du Buisson, another prisoner, was standing in the King's Bench coffee room with his back to the fire. Bowes ordered him to move, and told him that if he did not he would throw a porter pot at his head. A scuffle ensued in which Bowes broke du Buisson's teeth. In the following year there was a serious riot in the prison, caused by disappointment at the throwing out of a Bill 'For the Relief of

The Unhappy Countess

Insolvent Debtors, etc.' This time Bowes came out strongly on the side of the authorities; was appointed chairman of the prisoners' association; presented a clock for the prisoners' benefit; and when, in June, 1796, Mr. Thomas Erskine once more appeared for him in Court, he was able to tell the Judge that his client had been in prison for ten years and that the Marshal of the King's Bench would testify to the strict propriety of his conduct.

This was the year in which he appealed unsuccessfully to the House of Lords against the Lord Chancellor's decree; but the edge was taken off his disappointment by the hatching of an entirely new and most promising chancery suit.

On December 10th Bowes petitioned the Lord Chancellor to declare that he was entitled to a third share of two farms in County Durham, Mount Farm and Spring Farm, properties which had been bought by George Bowes in partnership with two of his fellow coal-owners. This transaction had taken place *after* the signing of George Bowes' will in 1747 and *before* the signing of a codicil to that will; and Stoney Bowes' claim was based on a legal quibble and on yet another 'deed of revocation', the existence of which he had forgotten all about owing, as he claimed, to 'distress of mind'.

The legal quibble turned on the question as to whether the codicil did or did not constitute a republication of George Bowes' will. If it did, then Bowes' share in these two farms would follow the will trusts and would be subject to the deeds of January 9th and 10th, 1777. If it did not, then these properties were excluded from the trusts, and on this assumption Bowes produced a 'deed of lease and release', signed by Lady Strathmore in November, 1781, by which her share in the two farms had been assigned to a county Durham solicitor, George Pearson, 'to hold for the use of Andrew Robinson Bowes and his heirs and assigns for ever'. The revenue from these properties from 1781 was claimed, on behalf of Bowes, from the Receiver of Lady Strathmore's estates.

The transaction of December, 1781, was, to say the least of it, a fishy one. Pearson, a solicitor of no great reputation, was dead. One of the witnesses of Lady Strathmore's signature, Dr. James Scott, rector of Simonburn in Northumberland, could remember nothing about the business at all, and doubted if he had ever witnessed the document in question. Lady Strathmore declared that she had been so frightened of Bowes that she had signed any papers that he had put in front of her.

This new chancery suit dragged on; and in 1798 an issue of law was referred to the judges of the Court of King's Bench, who certified: 'We have heard counsel in this case and we are of the opinion that the codicil was not a republication of the will so as to extend the operation of the will to the real estate purchased after the will was executed. It extends to estates devised by the will and no further.' In short, the issue was decided in Bowes' favour. In the following year Bowes petitioned that the third share in the farms should be handed over to him; and again he won his case. Lord Strathmore and his mother appealed to the House of Lords, who dismissed the appeal. This was Bowes' first major legal triumph.

Indeed, for the moment, things seemed to be going his way, for in the previous year he had successfully appealed against bankruptcy proceedings brought against him by the unlucky Peacock, it having been ruled by the Court of Chancery that Bowes, though he had an interest in four collieries at Benwell and was part-owner of a coal ship, was not a trader under the meaning of the bankruptcy laws, the Lord Chancellor observing that it had been decided that a part-owner could not be a bankrupt—'Men of the first rank,' he declared, 'were concerned in India ships, and the effect would be that half the House of Lords would be liable to the Bankruptcy Law if a commission could be taken out against a part-owner.'

Lady Strathmore's death in 1800 must also have stimulated and encouraged him; and thanks to the efforts of his latest attorney, Mr. Palmer, 'who undertook by a sort of tontine to fill up the requisite securities for his debts to the satisfaction of the Marshal', Bowes moved out of the King's

The Unhappy Countess

Bench prison and was permitted by the Marshal to live in a house in London Road, St. George's Fields, 'within the prison rules'. Foot reports that he took with him Miss Sutton, her children and all his cats and dogs 'of which he had more than a common share and which he kept very poor'. He was still up to his old tricks, both amatory and legal. He rented a second house in London Road in which he installed 'a very neat and modest young woman, a sempstress, who had visited her sister in the King's Bench prison who was associated with a gentleman there, a clergyman'. On one of Jenny Sutton's rare absences from home, Bowes tried to transfer his new lady love to his own house. This move was defeated by the Sutton children; and the ex-sempstress having given birth to a child, Bowes settled money on her and persuaded her to swear the child on a prisoner in the Bench.

The finding of the House of Lords in the matter of the Mount Farm and Spring Farm properties still stood; but Lady Strathmore's death had complicated the issue and the third share which Bowes had successfully claimed was not handed over to him. In 1802 he again applied to the Court of Chancery; and in 1806 the issue of law was once more threshed out in the Court of Common Pleas, Lord Strathmore claiming, as executor of his mother's will, that the deed of lease and release of December, 1781, had been obtained by duress. It was the old story of the deed of revocation all over again; and for the last time the Court had to hear the whole sorry story of Bowes' relations with his wife. The brief prepared for Lord Strathmore's counsel ('Mr. Hullock, Mr. Serj. Cockell, Mr. Serj. Best and Mr. Holroyd with you', modestly marked 20 gns.) is still in existence. It is a long and remarkable document.

The jury found that the deed had been obtained by duress —and Bowes' last, his very last, hope of getting his hands on at least a fragment of the Bowes property vanished for ever.

In 1804 one of his sisters had come over from Ireland to pay him a visit. Bowes, true to form, had pretended to be seriously ill, had sworn that Jenny Sutton was vicious, unfeeling and abandoned, and had shown his sister a will in which she figured as a legatee. His object had been to extract some ready money from his brother-in-law. The brother-in-law had disappointed his expectations. His debtors began to get clamorous; and Bowes dreaded the possibility of a return within the prison walls. He lost his usual hearty appetite, and in his daily walk he got no further than a nearby tavern where he used to read a newspaper. The only book in his house was a much thumbed copy of Lady Strathmore's *Confessions*. Foot declares, 'I do not believe he ever read a single book through, from the first hour he went to prison, to the very last.' He kept no servants, and refused to buy brushes or brooms. 'The two daughters went down upon their knees and gathered up the dust with their hands.' He allowed Jenny Sutton only one meal a day, and scarcely ever spoke to her.

On January 10th, 1810, Foot was summoned to his house. For the first time in all his professional visits, Jenny Sutton opened the door. Bowes had cried wolf all too often, but this time Foot was of the opinion that he had not long to live. Jenny Sutton, in great distress, explained that he had recently made a new will in which she was left nothing. Foot said he would see what he could do. 'The next morning,' Foot writes, 'I called at Lincoln's Inn and saw Mr. Robbins, Mr. Meredith [Bowes' current attorney] being out of town. I told Mr. Robbins all the circumstances of my call. He appointed me to meet him at Bowes' house; he took a gentleman with him. On our coming, we found there a sister of Bowes, just arrived in London from Ireland. Here also came into our company Mr. Sampson Perry, who had been attending Bowes in a friendly and medical capacity for some time previous to this dangerous state.

'All being now assembled, as if from sympathy, all were devoted to see if Bowes could be prevailed upon to give anything to Miss Sutton. It ought not to be omitted that Bowes' sister, from the goodness of her heart, had at her own expense called in the clergyman of the parish. With these powerful engines; with the particular address of Mr. Sampson Perry, with the intercession of all around him, with the begging of the children, advancing to the bedside one after the other, Bowes at length gave way, opened his mouth, and consented to Miss Sutton having one hundred pounds per annum. This being avowed to Mr. Perry by Bowes, and legally put down by Mr. Robbins, witnessed by him, his friend and myself, we took our leave. I ought to observe there was not a shilling in the house, till Mr. Robbins left a sum . . . a ready display of direct humanity upon this necessitous occasion.'

Bowes died six days later, on January 23rd, 1810, and was buried in the vault of St. George's Church in the Borough.

Foot is severe in his summing up of his character. 'His ruin was finally precipitated from want of moral principle and personal courage. If he had happened to have been a man of courage, as well as infamy, he would, with his talent, have maintained that which infamy alone had put into his possession; and he would have mounted instead of sunk . . . but his mind was treacherous and inconstant even to itself. He was a villain to the backbone!

'In every turn of his affairs, his passion indicated all the sufferings of a coward, without the smallest show of fortitude.

'. . . To sum up his character in a few words, he was cowardly, insidious, hypocritical, tyrannic, mean, violent, selfish, jealous, revengeful, inhuman and savage, without a single countervailing quality. Let us hope when he departed, that never before nor since there never was, nor ever will be, taking him for all in all, his parallel.'

CHAPTER EIGHT

The Tenth Earl

It is an agreeable change to turn from Lady Strathmore and Stoney Bowes to the contemplation of John, 10th Earl of Strathmore. Lady Strathmore's eldest son may not have been a pillar of respectability, but he was an exceptionally handsome, good-natured, intelligent man who loved beautiful things, especially women and thoroughbred horses; and above all he was kind.

He had had a wretched childhood, first neglected and disliked by his mother and then bullied by his uncle-guardian, Thomas Lyon. From his private school at Neasden he went to Edinburgh High School. From Edinburgh he went to Caen in Normandy; and from Caen to Cambridge. On coming down from Cambridge he joined the Royal Regiment of Oxford Blues, and had his portrait painted in his handsome uniform. In 1790 he came of age and, as has already been related, purchased his mother's life interest in the Gibside and Streatlam Castle properties. Independent and rich, he found himself happy for the first time in his life; and almost at once he fell in love.

The object of his affections was a married woman, Lady Tyrconnel.

Sarah Tyrconnel was born in 1763, the daughter of Sir John Hussey Delaval, Bart.—later the 1st Lord Delaval—of Seaton Delaval in Northumberland. There is a portrait of Sarah Delaval—'Hussey' as her family called her—painted when she was eight years old and already an assured beauty with pale gold hair. 'I can always,' she announced, 'get exactly what I want from Papa.' In 1779, when she was sixteen, she was married to George Carpenter, 2nd Earl of Tyrconnel, a friend of her father who had parted from his wife. She was wild and unreliable, but she had great beauty and extraordinary vitality. In 1787 she fell in love with Frederick, Duke of York; and her father bought Claremont, near Esher—ostensibly to provide a country seat for his impoverished son-in-law but in reality to provide his adored 'Hussey' with a house near her lover, who lived at Oatlands. In 1788 Sir Nicholas Wraxhall noted that the Duke of York was 'held by a lady, feminine and delicate in her figure, very fair, with a profusion of light hair in the tresses of which, like the tangles of Neaera's in *Lycidas*, His Royal Highness was detained captive'. When Lady Tyrconnel rode, her hair 'floated on the saddle'. In 1790 the Duke of York ended the romance by marrying the daughter of the King of Prussia, and that Christmas Lady Tyrconnel persuaded her father to entertain a large party at Seaton Delaval to witness the presentation of *The Fair Penitent* by the Delavals and their friends. Lady Tyrconnel played the part of Calista, the lovely and faithless wife who, repenting of her adultery, stabs herself on her lover's bier. It was a gesture of renunciation which the Delavals fully appreciated.

The Fair Penitent was played again in February, and on this occasion Mr. Henry Swinburne, author of *The Courts of Europe*, happened to be present. He was critical of the amateur caste. 'Lord Delaval', he wrote, 'was correct and pathetic as Sciotto, Lady Tyrconnel mumbled her phrases, but looked the thing. Lord Tyrconnel as Lothario was too bulky, his coat too scanty, and he sawed the air overmuch.'

Soon afterwards Lord Strathmore dined with Henry Swinburne, who had a house in County Durham not far from Gibside, and, fired by the account of this gifted but rackety family, he asked his host if it would be possible to get him an invitation to the next theatrical performance. The invitation was forthcoming and John Strathmore, now twenty-two, accompanied Swinburne to Seaton Delaval where they were 'most hospitably received, the play was even better acted by Lord Delaval and his daughters, and on account of the darkness of the night, the company stayed until eight in the morning'. A few weeks later Henry Swinburne, not perhaps altogether pleased, wrote to a friend, 'I found on my return to this part of the country that my entertainment of Lord Strathmore at Seaton Delaval had been followed up, and that he was now completely *domicilié* in the family. The whole party sent to ask me to sup with them after the Guild Ball at the inn at Newcastle. I was rather surprised to see the intimacy which had struck up so suddenly, and a fine scene between Lady Tyrconnel and Lord Strathmore afforded me great amusement. The poor man is desperately smitten. I was invited to a third performance in which he was to take part.'

Given the circumstances of his lonely upbringing, 'Hussey' was just the kind of woman with whom the romantic John Strathmore would, inevitably, have fallen in love.

That October, a paragraph in *The Star*, duly cut out and pasted into his mother's album, announced that 'the Earl and Countess of Tyrconnel, attended by the young Earl of Strathmore, the Misses Daniel etc.' had spent ten days viewing the various spectacles of the different Westmorland lakes and the surrounding mountains.

In the summer of 1792 Lord Strathmore bought Claremont Lodge, within a mile or so of Claremont House; and to Claremont Lodge, with the amenable Lord Tyrconnel as his racing partner, he moved such of the thoroughbreds at the Streatlam stud as had survived his step-father's régime. But in the midst of these preoccupations he never forgot his brothers and sisters. Mrs. Bland, that arch purveyor of gossip, wrote to 'her dear Miss Heber' on February 16th, 1793, 'Lady Anne Jessup & her family have been staying some time with her mother, but they have had a fall out, so Lord Strathmore has taken them all to him & at present they are staying with Lady Tyrconnel—"*Merry Companions every one*".' John Strathmore always came to the rescue, in however unorthodox a fashion.

He and Lady Tyrconnel were inseparable. At a race

meeting at Gibside 'Hussey' gave away the prizes. He played the part of Cassio in a performance of *Othello* at Seaton Delaval. Even the broadminded Lord Delaval became perturbed, noting that he had 'written to Hussey from Doncaster in strong terms'. There was also growing concern about her health. From Gibside, in 1798, she wrote to her father, 'I continue to keep very good hours and take proper riding and walking exercise, though the former is only about the place, for the roads are awful.'

She had contracted consumption. The summer of 1800 was exceptionally hot. On August 8th Dr. Abbs was called to Seaton Delaval where Lady Tyrconnel and Lord Strathmore were staying. On August 15th Lord Delaval noted, 'Abbs said there was no reason to suppose that the state of her illness should prove incurable by *digitalis* when it had been found capable of curing cases of the lungs infinitely worse than hers.' But her condition worsened. She went to her father's London house in Portland Place, and then went north again to Gibside which had become, in every sense, her second home. And at Gibside, early in October, 1800, she died.

An effort was made to hush up the fact that she had died in her lover's house. A discreet if misleading obituary notice, said to have been written by Lord Delaval himself, appeared in *The Newcastle Chronicle* of October 11th: 'Died, Tuesday last, at Seaton Delaval, inconsolably lamented by her family and deeply regretted by all who knew her, the Countess of Tyrconnel, after a severe illness of many months which she bore with such patience and resignation as could only have been supplied by her inimitable suavity of temper and the truest sense of religion.' *The Gentleman's Magazine* bluntly stated that the Countess had died at Gibside; and Augustus Hare, who was a great-grandson of Lady Anne Simpson, writes in *The Story of My Life:* 'Gibside had two ghosts, one, "in a silk dress", being that Lady Tyrconnel who died in the house while living there on somewhat too intimate terms with John, Earl of Strathmore. He gave her a funeral which almost ruined the estate. Her face was painted like the most

JOHN, 10TH. EARL OF STRATHMORE

THE MAUSOLEUM CHAPEL, GIBSIDE

brilliant life. He dressed her head himself! and then, having decked her out in all her jewels, and covered her with Brussels lace from head to foot, he sent her up to London, causing her to lie in state at every town upon the road, and finally to be buried in Westminster Abbey!'

Lady Tyrconnel was thirty-seven when she died, six years older than John Strathmore. She must have been a bewitching creature. Dean Stanley referred to her as 'the wildest of her race'—and that, for a Delaval, was saying quite a lot. She is said to have appeared naked to the waist on a hot summer's day in the presence of an austere judge. She had completely entranced and enslaved the impressionable John Strathmore. He had adored her, and he never got over her death.

Broken-hearted he went to stay at Seaton Delaval and there he embarked on a sad, ill-judged, and rather humiliating love affair with 'Hussey's' daughter, Lady Susannah —or Susan—Carpenter.

Mrs. Bland, writing to Miss Heber on November 3rd, 1801, could not resist an unkind dig: 'This place had disposed of Lord Strathmore to Lady —— Carpenter, Daughter to his favourite Lady Tyrconnel. I hope she is too old to be nearly related to him.'

It was true that Lord Strathmore was attracted to this girl, but it was an attraction attended by heart-searchings and doubts. Mrs. Fenton Cawthorne described his courtship in a letter to her brother, Lord Delaval. 'The fascinated Lord Strathmore stared at her intently, seemed to be on the point of making some declaration, only to withdraw so abruptly that she was quite put out of countenance by his apparent rudeness.' Finally he brought himself to propose, and Lady Susan, who was every bit as spoilt and indulged by her family as her mother had been, at first accepted him and then thought better of it.

To escape from an embarrassing situation Susan Carpenter went to stay with Mrs. Cawthorne, who again wrote to her brother. '. . . I was in hope that my dear niece had seen the folly of her whimsical temporizing and had finally concluded upon a step which I think would ensure her happiness. I believe I have scarcely had credit in my observations of the caprice and whim of my niece since she has been under my care. I am still firmly persuaded it is my niece's determination to marry Lord Strathmore.'

Lady Susan thought otherwise. On her return to Seaton Delaval she wrote to her aunt: '. . . I am quite astonished you should talk of my determination to marry Lord Strathmore, and must beg you to re-peruse my letter in which you will find nothing of the kind. Indeed, after his lordship's conduct, I feel it impossible to renew any engagement as I should have very little certainty of happiness in uniting myself to a person who said such cruel things to me and who treated me for three months with such marked neglect.'

It was not in Lord Strathmore's nature to be unkind or neglectful. He must have been horribly torn between memories and longings.

Lord Tyrconnel was against the match; there was a long correspondence about returning some Strathmore diamonds; and in 1805 Lady Susan married Henry, 3rd Marquess of Waterford.

For consolation, John Strathmore turned, as his grandfather before him had turned, to Gibside and to his thoroughbred stud at Streatlam Castle.

Employing it is thought David Stevenson of Newcastle upon Tyne as his architect, he re-built the old Blakiston house, removing the top storey, adorning the south front with a high battlemented parapet pierced with outsize cross-shaped oeillets, and reconstructing the original porch. The sympathetic respect for Jacobean architecture which his operations display was unusual at the beginning of the nineteenth century. It might have been expected that he would have re-built Gibside in the prevailing taste of the day.

His grandfather's landscape layout was in ruins, for the beech woods that clothed the steep river bank had been ruthlessly felled by Stoney Bowes who boasted that he had paid for two elections by felling the Gibside timber and that if he stood again—as was his intention if he had won his case —he would have raised the money by cutting the brush-wood.

John Strathmore re-planted the policies, his beeches standing until they were felled just before the Second World War; and in one important respect he completed his grandfather's self-imposed task of making Gibside the finest place in the North. After George Bowes' death a good deal of work had been done on the mausoleum chapel, designed by James Paine, which was to be the crowning feature of the landscape. The structure had probably been completed and the building roofed, but the interior had not been decorated nor had any furnishings been provided—presumably the £8,000 left by George Bowes in his will for the chapel's completion had been exhausted and no one had chosen to expend any more money on the undertaking. John Strathmore made most handsome amends. He and his architect had a magnificent shell on which to work and when, in 1812, the chapel was at last finished and dedicated, and when George Bowes' coffin had been brought from Whickham parish church and laid in its niche in the crypt, that man of excellent taste would surely have been delighted with his grandson's achievement. He would also have been pleased by Christopher Hussey's description of his chapel in *Country Life*: '. . . this building deserves to be known for what it is, the masterpiece of its designer and one of the most exquisite works of English classical architecture, although it is no more than a fragment of the majestic landscape conception of which it formed the culmination.'

At Esher, and later, after Lady Tyrconnel's death, at Streatlam, Lord Strathmore resuscitated his grandfather's thoroughbred stud which, like everything else, had been allowed to run to seed by Stoney Bowes. In 1792 he had bought Queen Mab, by Eclipse out of the Tartar Mare, who became the dam of the Doncaster Cup winner Oberon and of Remembrancer, who won the St. Leger for her owner in 1803. Queen Mab became the foundation mare of the Streatlam's stud second period of greatness. In 1800 he bought the filly foal Vicissitude. He trained as well as bred at Streatlam, and it is said that still in the park a ribbon of greener turf can be faintly seen where John Smith worked his master's horses. Gibside Fairy, a daughter of Hermes and Vicissitude, foaled at Streatlam in 1811, was to help found the fortunes of his son's phenomenal successes on the Turf.

Again like his grandfather he interested himself in politics. As soon as he had come of age he had stood for election as a representative Scottish peer. He was not elected at his first attempt, but he was successful in 1796, and again in 1802 and in 1807.

2

Augustus Hare, in *The Story of My Life*, re-telling the legend as it had been related to him by his mother, slightly bowdlerizes and considerably confuses the strange story of Lord Strathmore's marriage. 'John, Earl of Strathmore,' he writes, 'was a very agreeable and popular man, but by no means a moral character. Living near his Castle at Streatlam was a beautiful girl named Mary Milner, daughter of a market-gardener at Staindrop. With this girl he went through a false ceremony of marriage, after which, in all innocence, she lived with him as his wife. Their only boy, John Bowes, was sent to Eton as Lord Glamis. On his death-bed Lord Strathmore confessed to Mary Milner that their marriage was false and that she was not really his wife. She said, "I understand that you mean to marry me now, but that will not do; there must be no more secret marriages"; and, ill as he was, she had everyone within reach summoned to attend the ceremony, and she had him carried to church and was married to him before all the world. Lord Strathmore died soon after he re-entered the house, but he left her Countess of Strathmore. It was too late to legitimatize John Bowes.'

The true story, as it was related in great detail in the course of the hearing of the Strathmore Peerage claim before the Committee of Privileges of the House of Lords, is a good deal stranger than that, and redounds a good deal more to the credit of both Mary Milner and Lord Strathmore.

Mary Milner was born at Stainton (not Staindrop), Co. Durham, in 1787. Lord Strathmore first saw her in 1809 at Wemmergill Hall, his shooting box on the Yorkshire moors. She was asked in the witness box in what capacity she had been living at Wemmergill. Her counsel objected to the question, and it remained unanswered; but it is believed that she was employed as a housemaid. There was no 'false ceremony of marriage' and Mary Milner never had any reason to suppose that she was married to her protector. Having lived with her for some time at Wemmergill, he installed her in a house in Paradise Row, Chelsea. In June, 1811, she moved to lodgings in South Street, Chelsea, and there gave birth to a son who, on June 29th, was baptized and was entered in the register as 'John Bowes, son of John and Mary Milner'. The midwife who attended the birth testified that Lord Strathmore had visited the mother soon after the child was born and had 'seemed very pleased it was a boy'. Lord Strathmore was present at the christening and executed a codicil to his will bequeathing £10,000 in trust for his son, or reputed son, John Bowes Milner. When the boy was a year old Mary Milner took him to Wemmergill Hall. A year later they both moved to Streatlam Castle. In 1817 they were installed in Lord Strathmore's London house in Conduit Street, and his lordship, who had recently been created Baron Bowes in the Peerage of the United Kingdom, made a new will in which he left all his English estates 'to my son, or reputed son, who is now called or known by the name of John Bowes'.

The 'Milner' had been dropped, and as John Bowes he was sent to a fashionable private school at Ealing kept by the Rev. William Goodenough.

'Did you ever sit at the head of his Lordship's table?' Mary Milner was asked at one of the hearings of the Committee of Privileges.

The Unhappy Countess

'I did. I dined with him always and sat at the head of his table.'

'When his Lordship had company?'

'No.'

She added that she had never accompanied Lord Strathmore to Gibside.

A letter which Lord Strathmore wrote to his son has survived.

WEMMERGILL
18th August 1819.

MY DEAR BOY,

By this day's Mail Coach I have sent from Brough a box containing three brace of Moor Game which you will present to Mr. and Mrs. Goodenough with my best compliments. I have enclosed a copy of the directions of the box, that you may know where enquiry is to be made in case any unnecessary delay should take place in its arrival . . . I am happy to hear from Mr. Goodenough so favourable an account of you, and trust that you will continue to merit his approbation.

I remain, my dear Son,
Your affectionate Father,
BOWES STRATHMORE.

He was proud of the boy, and very fond of him.

In the following year, when John Bowes was still at school at Mr. Goodenough's, Lord Strathmore fell seriously ill with 'dropsy and water on the chest'. He was confined to bed, suffered excruciating pain, and was nursed devotedly by Mary Milner. At 4 o'clock in the morning of Saturday, July 1st, he sent for Mr. John Dean Paul, a banker who had married Lady Anne Simpson's daughter. He informed Mr. Paul that he wished to marry Mary Milner with whom he had lived for so many years, and asked him to obtain a special licence so that the ceremony could take place not in a church but in his own Conduit Street house. Mr. Paul at once made application to the Archbishop of Canterbury; but the Archbishop, who knew how matters stood, refused to grant a special licence. Mr. Paul then applied to Doctors'

Commons for a licence for the celebration of marriage in the common form of the church, and this was granted.

The marriage was celebrated next morning, July 2nd, at 8 a.m. in St. George's Church, Hanover Square. The service was taken by the rector, the Very Reverend Robert Hodgson who, a few weeks before, had been installed in the Deanery of Carlisle. Besides the bride and bridegroom, the only other people present were Henry Jadis, Henry Uhthoft, and two menservants from Conduit Street. Henry Jadis, a close friend of Lord Strathmore, was the son of Sophie Delaval, Lady Tyrconnel's sister; and Uhthoft was Lord Strathmore's solicitor.

Lord Strathmore was carried from his bedroom by the menservants, placed in a sedan chair, carried to the church, and set down 'as near the altar rails as the chair could approach'.

In the course of the hearing of the subsequent Peerage case the Dean of Carlisle was challenged as to the validity of the ceremony. He knew, the Dean said, all about the circumstances of the case. He was aware that the Archbishop had refused to grant a special licence—the granting of such a licence, he pointed out, was an act of grace, and the Archbishop's action in no way affected his own decision to conduct the ceremony. He had been determined to take the service himself, so that, if there was any blame attaching, the fault would be his and not that of one of his curates.

He had insisted, he told the Committee of Privileges, on Lord Strathmore 'coming out of the sedan chair and standing where the service required him to stand, and kneeling where it required him to kneel'. When he reached the question as to whether there was any legal impediment, he stopped the service, went up to Lord Strathmore, and asked him whether he was perfectly conscious of what was passing at the time and whether he came there with his own free will and consent. He had asked these questions, he explained, in order to determine whether Lord Strathmore was in a sane state of mind. Lord Strathmore said he had come with his own unbiased judgment, with his own free will and consent, and it would be one of the happiest moments of his life. The Dean had therefore proceeded with the ceremony. Lord Strathmore had made every response distinctly, had thanked him afterwards, and said that he had derived great comfort from what had passed. He had signed the Register. 'It appeared to me,' the Dean declared, 'he was in a perfectly sane state of mind and perfectly competent to decide for himself as to the service in which he was engaged.' Asked whether his Lordship was bodily *in extremis*, the Dean replied, 'Very weak; but how could I tell if *in extremis*? No, I didn't think him *in extremis*. I think that no man who had such a voice as he had could be said to be *in extremis*.' Pressed further, the Dean admitted that Lord Strathmore had been supported on either side by his friends when he had stood; but insisted that when he had knelt, 'he had both his knees upon the cushion'.

Lord Strathmore was carried back from the church to Conduit Street; and a note was immediately sent to the Rev. William Goodenough at Ealing informing him that his pupil, John Bowes, was now Lord Glamis.

At 2 a.m. on the following day, July 3rd, Lord Strathmore died.

His body was taken for burial to the crypt of the chapel at Gibside; and at the Bowes Museum there is a letter written to Mr. John Dean Paul by Lady Anna Maria Jessup.

BIRD HILL,
July 7th, 1820.

As I find from you that the dear Boy is with his mother to follow my beloved Brother to the grave, my daughter and myself have also determined to show him this last mark of our sincere affection, and as I wish to do any and every thing which I think would gratify him could he witness my actions, we intend going to Gibside on the 18th to receive him. . . . It will afford us the most consolation I am capable of receiving; to keep up an intercourse with the dear Child is what I most earnestly wish and desire. . . . My dear and lamented Brother has chosen the same magnanimity of mind in his last hours as he has done through life.

3

Immediately after the death of the 10th Earl, the Hon. Thomas Bowes, Mary Eleanor's third but only surviving son, claiming that he was the true and legitimate heir male of his father, the 9th Earl, assumed the title of Earl of Strathmore and Kinghorne, and 'finding that persons who supported John Bowes claimed for him the Earldom of Strathmore, petitioned His Majesty'.

Through James Farrer, his next friend—this much-tried lawyer was now living in retirement in Bath—John Bowes claimed that, thanks to the marriage of his parents on July 2nd, he 'had thereby obtained the character and status of a legitimated child *per subsequens matrimonium*; that he is, therefore, a legitimate son, and the true heir male of the 10th Earl'.

The boy's advisers at first contented themselves with claiming for him the Scottish dignities. He later petitioned that he was also entitled to the United Kingdom barony of Bowes, granted to his father in 1815.

'It fell on John Bowes,' as his uncle's lawyers grimly stated, 'to establish these arduous legal positions.'

A very great deal was at stake. In the first place, the legitimacy or illegitimacy of John Bowes depended on the result of the claim. Under the law of Scotland, the doctrine of *per subsequens matrimonium* ensured that children born out of wedlock were legitimized by the subsequent marriage of their parents. No such relief was then afforded by the law of England. If it could be proved that John Bowes was in fact the son of the 10th Earl and of Mary Milner, that the marriage of July 2nd had been a valid marriage, and that the 10th Earl and Mary Milner had had a Scottish domicile— then John Bowes would be declared the legitimate son of his father and would be entitled to succeed in his claim not only to the family honours but also to the entailed Scottish estates which, at this time, brought in £12,000 a year. If, on the other hand, it could be proved by the other side either that John Bowes was not the son of the 10th Earl and Mary

The Unhappy Countess

Milner, or that the marriage of July 2nd was invalid, or that the 10th Earl and Mary Milner had had an English and not a Scottish domicile, then John Bowes would be declared illegitimate, and his uncle, Thomas Bowes, would succeed both to the family honours and to the Scottish estates. The English estates, worth £20,000 a year, would come to John Bowes in any case under the terms of his father's will.

The petitions were heard by the Committee of Privileges in April and May, 1821.

Thomas Bowes' claim was heard first. On his behalf it was maintained that his grandfather, the 8th Earl of Strathmore, from the time of his marriage to Jane Nicholson, had resided principally on his wife's estates in County Durham; that his father, the 9th Earl, had been born and brought up in England and, having married Mary Eleanor Bowes, heiress to the Streatlam Castle and Gibside estates, had obtained very great accessions to his own English properties and had resided almost entirely in County Durham or in London; and that his brother, the 10th Earl, had been born in London and, save for a spell at Edinburgh High School, had spent his boyhood and youth in England. In 1790 the 10th Earl had purchased his mother's life interest in the Gibside and Streatlam properties and, despite the fact that he had been elected a representative Scottish peer, had interested himself exclusively in his English estates, adding to them by purchase while selling land in Scotland. He had paid only occasional visits to Glamis which had been occupied by his factor and the factor's numerous family; and that the grass of the park had been allowed to grow right up to the door of the Castle. In 1815 he had been created a Peer of the United Kingdom. Mary Milner had been born in County Durham and had spent all her life in England.

In the light of these facts, Thomas Bowes' counsel argued, the 10th Earl could not claim Scottish domicile. 'A domicile of origin is that arising from a man's birth and connections . . . It is the preponderancy of incidents in a man's life and habits from the period of his birth, or at any rate from that of manhood, which fixes the point of his domicile.' They added that neither Mary Milner nor John Bowes had ever been to Scotland; and that John Bowes had been born in London and was at school in Ealing.

As regards the marriage of July 2nd, it was contended that even under Scottish law this ceremony would not have legitimized John Bowes because, when it had taken place, the 10th Earl had been *in articulo mortis*; and because, as his state of health would have prevented him from consummating the marriage, 'one of the essential duties for which the parties stipulated' could not have been fulfilled and it had not, therefore, been a true marriage.

Finally, it was argued that John Bowes could not be a lawful son in one country and a bastard in another; and that in the case of a marriage celebrated in England, a marriage contract must be covered by the law of England.

For John Bowes it was claimed that the 10th Earl had been a representative peer of Scotland, and that he had not at any time abandoned Glamis as one of his family seats. He had kept an establishment of servants there and he had invariably stayed in the Castle when he had visited Scotland. He could therefore have fairly claimed a Scottish domicile. It was emphasized—a point which was not strongly contested by the other side—that the 10th Earl had 'uniformly acknowledged' John Bowes as his son; and that the marriage of July 2nd had been valid because a marriage *in articulo mortis* was good so long as the mental faculties of the contracting party were entire (here the testimony of the Dean of Carlisle was of importance) and because canon law denied that consummation was an essential part of the contract if recovery from an incapacitating disease was possible—as it had been possible in the case of the 10th Earl. 'Admitting, therefore, that the marriage of the late Earl of Strathmore to Miss Milner did not legitimate the claimant in England, that is no reason why an English rule, inconsistent with the law of Scotland, and derogatory to the common law of all Europe besides, should operate beyond the territory of England and render the claimant incapable to succeed to the honours, offices and innumerable property situated in

Scotland when he possesses every quality necessary to create the legal character of an heir.'

But the Committee of Privileges found that the 10th Earl's domicile had been English and not Scottish; and that John Bowes' claim must fail.

4

This verdict could not, of course, affect the position of the new Countess Dowager of Strathmore, who had given her evidence at the enquiry with a dignity and a simplicity that impressed everyone who had heard her. In 1831 she married William Hutt, a man twenty years younger than herself who had been John Bowes' tutor; and with him she lived at Gibside until her death in 1860. Hutt, who was Member of Parliament for Hull from 1832 to 1841 and for Gateshead from 1841 to 1874, had a distinguished Parliamentary career, becoming Paymaster-General and Vice-President of the Board of Trade in one of Mr. Gladstone's administrations. He was made a Privy Councillor in 1860 and was created a Knight Commander of the Bath in 1865.

Augustus Hare, in *The Story of My Life*, draws one of his inimitable portraits of Lady Strathmore, with whom he stayed at Gibside shortly before she died:

'Lady Strathmore always behaved well. As soon as she was a widow, she said to all the people whom she had known as her husband's relations and friends that, if they liked to keep up her acquaintance, she should be very grateful to them, and always glad to see them when they came to her, but that she should never enter any house on a visit again; and she never did. . . . She was a stately woman, still beautiful, and she had educated herself since her youth, but, from her quiet life (full of unostentatious charity) she had become very eccentric. One of her oddities was that her only measurement of time was one thousand years. 'It is long since you have seen Mrs. Davidson?' I said. 'Yes, one thousand years.' 'Have you had your dog a long time?' 'A thousand years.'

172

'That must be a very old picture?' 'Yes, a thousand years old.'

'Seeing no one but Mr. Hutt, the agreeable tutor of her son, Lady Strathmore had married him, and by her wealth and influence he became member for Gateshead. He was rather a prim man, but could make himself very agreeable. He was vastly civil to me. I think he rather tyrannized over Lady Strathmore, but he was very well behaved to her in public.'

John Bowes was devoted to his mother; and as long as she lived the first thing he always did on returning to England from one of his frequent sojourns abroad was to go to Gibside to visit her.

CHAPTER NINE

John Bowes

THE 10th Earl's only son started life as John Bowes Milner; then he was known as John Bowes; for a day he was called Lord Glamis; for three months he was the 11th Earl of Strathmore; and after that he became plain John Bowes again.

As John Bowes he was sent to Eton, and from Eton he went to Trinity College, Cambridge, where W. M. Thackeray was one of his friends. From Cambridge, in 1828, he wrote a sensible letter to his solicitor in Barnard Castle explaining that if he kept two servants—one of them was a groom, young Isaac Walker—he must have £200 added to his yearly allowance. His trustees could well afford to meet this modest request, for large funds were accumulating during the minority of this very rich young man who had inherited the Gibside, the Streatlam Castle and the Yorkshire estates under the terms of his father's will.

He was very happy at Cambridge, where he began to ask questions about the coal trade and to take an interest in the Streatlam stud which was maintained until he came of age by his father's trustees, the produce being sold but not raced by them. He also developed a passion for acting and for private theatricals. When he was nineteen he bought his first picture—The Temptation of St. Anthony, then ascribed to Teniers but now given to Cornelius Saftleven. So the pattern of his life interests was already discernible—the coal trade, theatricals, the Streatlam thoroughbred stud, and picture buying.

In 1832 he came of age. On his twenty-first birthday a

chestnut colt was foaled at Streatlam, by Catton out of Emma, which was aptly named Mündig; three hundred tenants were entertained with roast beef and plum pudding; and three Ayrshire bullocks, weighing nearly eighty stone each, were killed and distributed to his poorer neighbours. As his mother had married William Hutt and as he had arranged that she should have the use of Gibside for her life, he himself settled down at Streatlam Castle, the great classic eighteenth-century mansion near Barnard Castle which William Blakiston Bowes, George Bowes' eldest brother, had begun to build in 1718 and which had been nearly but not quite completed at his death in 1721. Large and impressive with its stone cupolas and French-looking banded rustication, standing on a terrace and approached by a bridge spanning the Streatlam Beck, it was a strange and awkward house because Blakiston Bowes had had it built round, and enclosing, the walls of the old Castle.

Aged twenty-one, John Bowes was returned to the newly reformed House of Commons as one of the two members for South Durham, his colleague being Joseph Pease, the Quaker. In his nomination speech he declared: 'I will not here, in the enlightened town of Darlington, argue the question of national education. There are some who argue that the happiness of the community is depreciated with the advancement in knowledge of its members; but that is only the cry of those who wish to arrest the advance of liberty. I am a sincere friend to popular education. I am the most sincere friend to the greatest freedom of religious faith. I consider that a man, so long as his religious opinions—just as his opinions on any science—do not tend to influence his conduct in such a manner as to injure the rest of the community, should not be bound by any penal statute.' He was a nervous speaker, but he had evidently inherited his great-grandfather's Whig principles. Mr. Pease polled 2,273 votes; John Bowes 2,218; and their Tory opponent, Mr. Shafto, 1841.

His course seemed clear enough. He would live at Streatlam Castle, which he would complete and probably enlarge. He would most likely achieve minor Cabinet office. Apart from his agricultural rents from sixty thousand odd acres he would draw a large but fluctuating income from his coal-trade partnership with Lord Ravensworth and others in the still continuing 'Grand Allies'. Thanks to the firm foundations laid down by his father he would have a distinguished career on the Turf. He would collect pictures; and, in a more decorous fashion—as befitted a more decorous age —Streatlam Castle might come to rival the old Seaton Delaval as the scene of distinguished private theatricals. He would choose a suitable wife from among the daughters of his North Country neighbours, and found a prosperous dynasty.

None of these things came to pass in quite this way— which is the reason why John Bowes' life is such an interesting one.

As a very young man he discovered that he far preferred life in Paris to life in County Durham. He developed a professional—as opposed to an amateur—interest in the theatre. Although he represented South Durham for fifteen years, he cut no great figure in the House of Commons and thankfully abandoned his parliamentary career when he was thirty-six. And far from being an inactive member of a traditional coal-trade partnership he broke away from the Grand Allies in 1844 and, with Charles Mark Palmer, an ambitious and progressive man of business, he founded a new private company, John Bowes, Esq., and Partners, which operated twelve collieries in County Durham and in Northumberland, including a valuable new seam which extended under the policies of Gibside and which, incidentally, undermined his great-grandfather's banqueting house. John Bowes, Esq., and Partners became one of the most powerful colliery companies in the country; and in 1851 Palmer, with Bowes' backing, started a ship-building and iron company at Jarrow. Their first vessel, the *John Bowes*, a screw steamer of 465 tons designed to carry thirty keels of coal and to make thirty trips a year from Newcastle to London, was launched in 1852. Although he won the Derby four times and never despised a good bet on one of his own horses he was more interested in the yearlings he bred at Streatlam than in winning races. He never belonged to 'the racing set' and after 1853 seldom if ever attended a race meeting. He married a French actress; managed, and later bought, the Théâtre de Variétés in Paris; and from 1854 regarded his Paris house, No. 7 Rue de Berlin, as his real home. Collecting—pictures, porcelain, tapestries, furniture, books—became the ruling passion of his life and led to the foundation of the Bowes Museum.

Such a curious shift in emphasis from his expected life-pattern suggests a strong will and, perhaps, some inherent flaw—not in his character but in his ego.

John Bowes certainly had a strong will. He was hard-headed, efficient and with an eye always directed towards the main chance. He was meticulous in the management of his business interests and of his estates. Almost daily, when he was abroad, he wrote to his lawyer at Barnard Castle, Mr. Dickinson Holmes, and to his agent at Streatlam, Mr. Ralph John Dent. These letters, many of which are preserved at the Bowes Museum, are models of clear, precise instruction, tempered with a rather dry, pawky humour. His mode of addressing his correspondents was admirably consistent. To Mr. Dent he invariably began 'dear sir'; to Mr. Holmes 'my dear sir'. It would have taken a very early riser to have got the better of him, and it was said that he possessed the useful faculty of being able to conceal from the person to whom he was talking all evidence of whether he liked him or not. He had no great aptitude for field sports, and he was not, as the term is now understood, a sportsman. In his own fashion—and only in his own fashion—he could be extremely generous.

He was a man of great practical and artistic ability who for some reason reacted against the kind of life and against the kind of society in which he would normally have found his interests and his friends. The reason may well have been his illegitimacy.

His failure to mix easily with his equals was especially marked in his career on the Turf. On the night of June 4th,

1832, so a well-known story runs, a thin, pale, dark, imperturbable young man walked through the dining-room of Crockford's and took a seat at the long table. It was the night of the Derby, so the room was crowded; but this newcomer, having ordered his dinner, betrayed not the slightest interest in the company, few of whom knew him by sight.

A member asked a club servant who he was.

'Don't you know, sir?' the club servant said. 'That is Mr. Bowes, whose Mündig won the Derby today.'

John Bowes, on this occasion, could have afforded to stand himself a good dinner, for he had backed his horse to win £20,000.

Mündig, ridden by William Scott and trained, as all Bowes' horses were trained, by John Scott, 'the Wizard of the North', at Whitewall, Malton, was a lucky winner; and a half-hearted attempt was made to label his owner 'Lucky Bowes'. If the nickname failed to stick, John Bowes and his all black racing colours inherited from his father—it was not until 1865 that he changed over to black and gold—remained for a time a highly successful owner; and under his direction the Streatlam stud enjoyed its third period of greatness. The first had been in the time of his great-grandfather, George Bowes. The second from 1790 until his father's death in 1820.

John Bowes' Turf successes were almost all achieved by the bloodstock bred at Streatlam, where the mares and yearlings grazed in paddocks surrounded by the high holly hedges planted by the stable lads in the time of the 10th Earl. Throughout his whole racing career Bowes seldom owned more than eight or nine brood mares at any one time, and the foundation mare of the Streatlam stud's third great period was Emma, by Whisker out of Gibside Fairy, whose progeny included Trustee, Mündig, Lady of Silverkeld, Cotherstone, As You Like It, and Mowerina. Altogether Emma had seventeen foals, with hardly a bad one among them.

Every autumn the yearlings at Streatlam were mustered, at first by old Isaac Walker, the stud groom, and later by his son, 'young' Isaac Walker, and the healthy and sound, usually numbering from three to six, were drafted to Malton, where their arrival was an annual event of considerable importance. John Scott would carefully assess their points and racing promise, assisted by his brother William, Frank Butler, Sim Templeman and Nat Flatman, while outside opinions were often obtained from such experts as Sir Tatton Sykes, Mr. Stanhope Hawke and Captain Bastard.

In 1837, no very promising yearlings having been bred at Streatlam, Mr. Bowes was told that a likely looking yearling was for sale at a Yorkshire farm. So the Whitewall gig was out and John Scott and his patron drove out to Stillington, where they found a bay yearling colt, by Brutandorf, almost as rough as a Shetland pony and running about a meadow with a half-bred colt which was so much bigger and heavier than the thoroughbred that the poor little bay was doing very badly. But John Scott bought the colt for Mr. Bowes for £100, and as Hetman Platoff he turned out to be one of the best horses the Whitewall stable ever had.

In 1839 Isaac Walker took old Emma all the way by road to Cheshire to visit Touchstone at the Eaton stud; and the resulting foal was Cotherstone. Cotherstone was a bad doer at first, but John Scott always fancied his chances, and a trial was arranged. William Scott, who was riding Cotherstone, finished third, and when he pulled up he decided to fool the touts and spies who always attended such trials by calling out to the boy to 'take the wretch away as he was worse than ever'. But he later told his brother and Mr. Bowes that the colt had exceptional merit.

Cotherstone won the 1843 Derby in a canter, and on this occasion, using Sir William Gregory as his 'commissioner', John Bowes collected £21,600 from the bookmakers.

Nine years later, in 1852, Bowes won his third Derby with a very moderate horse, Daniel O'Rourke, 'under fifteen hands, with neither good looks nor great merit and probably one of the worst Derby winners in history'. But in this same year a Streatlam-bred two-year-old called West Australian, by Melbourne out of Mowerina, was suspected of being a real phenomenon. He was the best horse that

Bowes ever owned and the best horse that John Scott ever trained, and in 1853 he won the Guineas, the Derby and the St. Leger—the first horse to gain the triple crown.

But by this time Mr. Bowes' interest in racing had already waned. He did not bother to go to Epsom to see West Australian's victory; and the 1853 Derby was to be his last classic win. He went on breeding thoroughbreds at Streatlam, but his appearances at race meetings became fewer and fewer. Frank Butler succeeded William Scott as the stable's first jockey, and Frank Butler, in his turn, was succeeded by the great Fordham. It was many years after Fordham's first engagement to ride Mr. Bowes' horses that the jockey set eyes on his master. One day at Newmarket Fordham was superintending the saddling of one of Mr. Bowes' horses when he noticed a stocky, grey-haired gentleman who was taking a marked interest in the process. Eventually the stranger made some observation about the horse's appearance. Fordham was by no means a man who permitted himself to be accosted by any idler in the crowd. His crusty rejoinder elicited the mild response, 'Oh, I am the owner of that horse.' It was said that Mr. Bowes was never seen on a racecourse again.

John Scott died in 1871, and Bowes set up Jem Perrin, who had for long been head man at Whitewall, as his private trainer; and each autumn the yearlings came up from Streatlam to Wold Cottage, Norton, and not, as before, to Whitewall. Right up to the day of his death, Bowes never had a thought of giving up racing; and through good fortune and bad he paid the Wold Cottage accounts without a murmur; but his luck had deserted him.

His failure—for it was viewed as such—to conform to the accepted pattern of a keen racing man was simply another manifestation of his shyness which may have caused him to be regarded—and much more importantly may have caused him to regard himself—as something of a bore. If a man does not make friends easily and if popularity appears to elude him, it is easy for him to seek an explanation and to find one; whereas the real answer lies in his own lack of self-confidence, in his failure or unwillingness to meet people half-way, and in forgetting that other people nearly always accept a man at his own valuation.

In Paris, and in the society of Parisian politicians, artists, musicians, and men and women of the theatre, John Bowes found an atmosphere and a climate which exactly suited him. No one there questioned his origins. He was rich, and he enjoyed figuring as a distinguished patron of the arts. Above all, in France, then as now, the arts were taken seriously.

He bought pictures regularly and with enthusiasm. In 1837 he had purchased the large 'Boar Hunt' by Snyders; a supposed Murillo, 'Beggar Boy'; a Carlo Maratti; a small Brekelenkamp; and a Cignani. He had commissioned J. F. Herring to paint some of his racehorses and the artist had given him two small pictures, 'Sheep' and 'Cattle'. In 1840 he bought twenty-three pictures, among them, at the Duke of Lucca's sale in London, the great 'Triptych of the Crucifixion' by the Master of the Virgo inter Virgines; the 'Miracle of the Holy Sacrament' by Sasseta; the 'St. Jerome' by Solario; and a 'St. Margaret' by Cignaroli. From Don Miguel of Portugal he bought the small triptych of the 'Deposition with Saints' by Ambrosius Benson; and pictures by Reynolds, Glover, Vernet, Santa Croce and Caprioli. In the following year he bought fourteen more important pictures including the Primaticcio 'Rape of Helen'; Salviati's 'Rape of the Sabines' (from the Queen Christina and the Duke of Orleans collections); a Francia; and a Nicolas Maes.

2

As early as 1832, the year in which John Bowes came of age, Thackeray had encountered his Cambridge friend in Paris, had dined with him on several occasions, and had 'talked about theatres'; and thereafter, whenever Thackeray was in Paris, references to dining or drinking tea with Bowes appear regularly in his letters, and Bowes financed one of his

The Unhappy Countess

less successful publishing ventures. But by 1849 these meetings had evidently begun to pall.

'I went to see Bowes,' Thackeray wrote in February of that year. 'He has 40,000 a year and palaces in the country, and here he is manager of the Théâtre de Variétés—and his talk was about actors and coulisses all the time of our interview—I wish it could be the last, but he has made me promise to dine with him and go I must to be killed by his melancholy GENTLEMANLIKENESS.'

Bowes may have been a dull companion in Thackeray's eyes; but it is also possible that the publication of Thackeray's *The Memoirs of Barry Lyndon Esq., Written by Himself*, which first appeared as a serial in *Fraser's Magazine* during 1844, had cast a shadow over their earlier friendship.

Barry Lyndon is not one of Thackeray's best novels; and its hero—or rather the gentleman-scoundrel who is its principal character and its only justification—was avowedly based on Andrew Robinson Bowes. After a long stay at Streatlam Castle in 1841, in the course of which he talked family history with his host and no doubt drew him out, Thackeray wrote to Fraser: 'I have in my trip to the country found materials (rather a character) for a story, that I'm sure will be amusing.' Internal evidence suggests that while he was at Streatlam he certainly read Jesse Foot's *Lives*. Whether Bowes was pleased by the re-publication of a by no means distant family scandal is open to question.

A comparison between the final chapters of *Barry Lyndon* and the true story of Stoney Bowes produces many close parallels, some significant differences, and a few passages which suggest that Thackeray may possibly have elicited some facts about his host's step-grandfather which are only hinted at in Foot's narrative.

Apart from the fact that they were both upstart Irish adventurers on the make, Barry Lyndon's—or rather Redmond Barry's—origins and early adventures in Ireland were presumably invented by their author; and Barry's participation in the Seven Years War and his enforced service with Frederick's Prussian Guards have no parallel in

Stoney Bowes' far more prosaic military career. But when Barry resolves that marriage must achieve his fortune, that 'anything is fair in love' and that 'men so poor as myself cannot afford to be squeamish about their means of getting on in life', and as soon as he selects as his victim the recently widowed Honoria, Countess of Lyndon—'the noblest and greatest heiress in England'—the parallels come thick and fast. Lady Lyndon had pretensions to being a bluestocking and a *bel esprit*—'Every adventurer who had a discovery in chemistry, or a plan for discovering the philosopher's stone, was sure to find a patroness in her.' She had a melancholy, deserted little boy, Viscount Bullingdon, who was looked after by her chaplain, Mr. Runt, with whom Barry is careful to make friends. Barry fights a duel with his rival, Lord George Poynings, and bribes a fortune-teller 'who did not fail to . . . describe as Lady Lyndon's future husband her persevering adorer, Redmond Barry Esq. This incident disturbed her very much.' Barry played on the countess's dislike of her family. 'The best friends I had in the prosecution of my tender suit were the countess's noble relatives; who were far from knowing the service they did me, and to whom I beg leave to tender my heartfelt thanks for the abuse with which they loaded me.'

He changed his name from Redmond Barry to Barry Lyndon. As his wife had only a life interest in her fortune he 'had to pay heavily for insuring her ladyship's life'. He cut down twelve thousand pounds' worth of timber on his wife's estates, encountering the protests of the young earl's guardians and meeting with considerable local opposition in the form of a refusal to buy the felled trees. He bought himself a property. He maltreated Lady Lyndon in every possible way, denied her society, bullied her into signing away her property, and spent her wealth in gambling. He was openly unfaithful to her and, when she complained, threatened to remove her children from her. He stood for Parliament and was returned. He angled in vain for an Irish peerage. His wife made desperate attempts to leave him; but he managed utterly to subdue her spirits. 'If I beckoned to her she would come fawning up to me like a dog.' He was trapped at last by her lawyers and was consigned to the Fleet prison, where he spent the last nineteen years of his life.

On the whole, the story of Barry Lyndon's marriage to Lady Lyndon is much weaker, duller and less dramatic than its real life counterpart. Thackeray tired of the book while he was writing it; and presumably felt some compunction in following Stoney Bowes' story too closely. But there are one or two passages which may have derived from intelligent and ingenious guesses on Thackeray's part or which, just conceivably, may have had their origin in something that he had been told by John Bowes—traditional stories handed down in the family.

Sir Charles Lyndon, Honoria's first husband, is speaking of his wife: 'She is a weak woman . . . you should see her, sir, how weak she is. . . . She has embittered my whole life. She is a fool; but she has got the better of one of the best heads in Christendom. She is enormously rich, but somehow I have never been so poor since I married her. . . . And she will do as much for my successor when I have gone.'

Was that the family version of the 9th Earl's feelings for his wife?

Then again the following passage may throw some light on how Stoney gained his ascendancy over Lady Strathmore.

'I saw her turn red and pale with fear and wonder, saw that my praise of her charms and the exposition of my passion were not unwelcome to her, and witnessed with triumphant composure the mastery I was gaining over her. Terror, to be sure, is not a bad ingredient of love. A man who wills fiercely to win the heart of a vapourish woman *must* succeed if he have opportunity enough . . . I found at length that the widow was growing dreadfully afraid of me; calling me her *bête noir*, her dark spirit, her murderous adorer. . . . My wish was to increase this sentiment of awe in her bosom, and to make her believe that I was a person from whom escape was impossible.'

And finally there is a curious reference to Barry Lyndon's flirtation with the World of Letters. It will be recalled that

John Bowes

William Scott, the future Lord Stowell, was at one time a close friend of Stoney's and an intimate of Doctor Johnson and a member of 'The Club'. It is tempting to imagine— though there is no proof of anything of the kind—that Scott may have introduced his raffish friend to the Doctor. Thackeray makes Barry Lyndon say:

'I had always a taste for men of letters, and perhaps, if the truth must be told, have no objection to playing the fine gentleman and patron among the wits. Such people are usually needy, and of low birth, and have an instinctive awe of a gentleman and a laced coat; as all must have remarked who have frequented their society. . . . It was through Mr. Reynolds that I was introduced to a score of these gentlemen, and their great chief, Mr. Johnson. I always thought their great chief a great bear. He drank tea twice or thrice at my house, misbehaving himself most grossly; treating my opinions with no more respect than those of a school-boy, and telling me to mind my horses and tailors, and not to trouble myself about Letters. . . .'

Invention on Thackeray's part, or—once again—something that John Bowes had told him? It is impossible to say.

Thackeray's visit to John Bowes at Streatlam Castle in the months of June and July, 1841, in the course of which the character of Barry Lyndon was conceived, did at all events produce an admirably vivid picture of the Streatlam household as it was when Bowes was living there as a bachelor; and of the South Durham election of 1841 in which Bowes participated.

It was customary at this date for a candidate at a general election to invite a journalist or literary friend to help him by composing election addresses or 'squibs'; and it was probably with this end in view that Bowes invited Thackeray to Streatlam.

With his tongue in his cheek, but with a wealth of acute observation sharpened by his unaccustomed surroundings, Thackeray wrote an account of his visit which appeared in the September and October 1841 numbers of *Fraser's Magazine* under the title of *Notes on the North What-d'ye-*

The Unhappy Countess

Callem Election. Being the Personal Narrative of Napoleon Putnam Wiggins, of Passimaquoddy.

In manner, this long contribution to *Fraser's* was a parody of the style of an American journalist, Nathaniel P. Willis; and Thackeray, in the guise of the mythical N. P. Wiggins, is supposedly recounting his experiences in a letter addressed to his aunt in Babylon, Kentucky, a relative from whom, as we are given to understand, he had considerable financial expectations.

Thackeray arrived at Streatlam Castle—and this is fact not fantasy—on the evening of Friday June 25th, and he stayed until July 13th. His account of his arrival and of the impressions which the castle made on him are all the more vivid because at that time staying in a large country house was a new experience for him. The smallest incidents, therefore, excited his interest; and he recounts them in fascinated detail.

He reached Darlington from York and drove out to Streatlam in a gig. A prim old lady swung the gates open, disclosing the long roads and avenues that traversed the park. A black Newfoundland, that kept up a huge yelling from his kennel under a sycamore, a St. Bernard dog and other hounds of smaller degree greeted him on his arrival at the house. John Bowes—or 'John Britton', as he features in the narrative—was away, and so, as Thackeray puts it, 'I was lord of a grand house and park, of a stable full of horses, a garden full of good things, and a hall full of servants.'

He develops this fantasy of temporary ownership to his heart's content. It evidently delighted him. A housekeeper met him on the steps with the words, 'You will dine, Sir?' and he was shown into a room with 'a great stiff shining damask table cloth, opposite which is placed a tall red chair. On the left hand side imagine a fire, such as they usually light here in the summer months, and containing at least three degenerated scuttlefuls of London coal. Opposite is an array of old plate, polished up to a pitch of supernatural brightness, flanked on each side by a decanter in a filigree stand. In the midst of this array is a jug of the commonest

186

earthenware—a 3*d.* yellow jug, inscribed "Britton for ever".'

His solitary dinner concluded, the old butler gave him his arm up a grand staircase 'to a tall tester bed, covered (for summer) with four blankets and a counterpane'. At 8 a.m. next morning 'a gentleman in black' brought him hot water in a jug with a Chinese landscape and figures on it, and his clothes (removed the previous evening by the valet) were returned neatly folded and elegantly brushed. 'Ditto boots.'

At 9 a.m. he breakfasted; and he describes the layout of the table:

'A clean table cloth and napkin, on it arranged:

	Eggs	
Dry toast		Hot cakes
	Butter	
Bread brown		Bread white
Cup Tea		Coffee Cup
Cream		Milk

'On the right of the plate, letters and newspapers. On the side table grilled ham, a silver mustard pot, a cold chicken, and a sort of pig's head jelly—very good indeed.' During the morning the temporary owner of Streatlam Castle read the newspapers and at 1 p.m. he was brought a tray of biscuits with a few lean slices of meat. After luncheon he sallied out to view 'his' house.

There were, he noted, twenty-four bedrooms, two oak drawing-rooms, a yellow drawing-room, a great dining-room—'with portraits of one's ancestors hanging on the walls'—a billiards room, a study, a gentlemen's room, etc. All the bedrooms were lofty, well carpeted, simple, furnished with sofas, reading chairs, and tables with writing books. Under each bed were half a dozen thick blankets.

There were colts and mares in the paddocks. The park stretched for miles, with long avenues of limes, firs and syca-mores. There was the beck, lined with rushes. In the garden there were hot walls—hollow walls, with flues running through them to facilitate the ripening of fruit; hot houses; great fat red-cheeked nectarines, basking in the sun; grapes just turning purple; 'a deal of flowers'.

Dinner was at 7 p.m., with 'amber sherry and lusty port'. After dinner he strolled in the park with a cigar, to the accompaniment of the braying of deer and the splashing of water, returning to drink a cup of tea.

Two hours after midnight, 'Mr. Britton' returned. He had been up since six that morning, had canvassed a score of villages, had driven a hundred miles, had not dined until 10 o'clock, and purposed to be off at 7 next morning, having ordered breakfast at 6.

At 6.30 his seconder and *aide de camp* cantered over the park on his black cob and made his appearance in a green coat and white duck pantaloons, with the 'Britton' colours. They sat down to a breakfast of muffins, eggs, grilled fowls and grilled ham, washed down with bowls of coffee and tea.

A carriage was waiting at the door with postillions and the galloping greys. It began to rain. 'It was curious and affecting almost, to see the perfect calmness and simplicity with which the postillions in their little green jackets and tight leathers bobbed regularly up and down as the celestial waters descended.' 'Mr. Britton' and his seconder lay back in their seats 'conning over in their minds the impromptus they are just going to make at Stuffington' (Darlington).

The account that Thackeray gives of the election is long and detailed and makes extremely good reading. But there have been plenty of accounts of nineteenth-century elections, and we may pass quickly over the villages with flags flapping over the ale houses and the women sporting the pink handkerchiefs, pink ribbons and pink gowns provided by the unscrupulous Tory candidate; the cavalcade that met 'Mr. Britton's' carriage at Stuffington; the ringing and chiming of the church bells; and the five hundred voters on horseback, each with a refreshment ticket entitling him to a free meal at the Sun Inn, which was 'Mr. Britton's' committee room— 'crowded with farmers, tradesmen, country gentlemen, doctors and a great power of lawyers'. 'Mr. Britton' appeared

on the balcony, took off his beaver hat and began to speak—
but thanks to Tory-organized hooliganism no one could hear
a syllable of what he said. At the luncheon (with toasts) that
followed, 'Mr. Britton' did not say a word in praise of himself,
only declaring that as long as he had health and the sinews
of war he would never allow a Pink to represent the famous
county. In the towns, it seems, the dissenters and manu-
facturers supported their class, and the people voted for the
popular, that is the Liberal, members. In the country
districts tenants on both sides voted with their landlords—
'when Farmer Jones said he was Squire Smith's tenant, as a
matter of course it was known that he would adopt Squire
Smith's colours'. Each village in the constituency was canvassed, and in every village each candidate had his own inn
or alehouse, with his flag at its door. There were placards,
squibs, songs and handbills; any number of dinners; and a
great scanning of election lists. On the two Polling Days a
system of horse-expresses brought to each committee room a
list of the voters as they polled. On the second day the High
Sheriff declared 'Lord George Cranley' (Lord Harry Vane)
and 'Mr. Britton' (John Bowes), duly elected as Knights of
the Shire, whereupon the Knights rode round the town and
rain fell in torrents. And that was that.

A curiously robust and earthy enterprise, perhaps, for the
John Bowes whose spiritual home was Paris; a more reasonable enterprise for the John Bowes who, in 1853, engaged in
a lengthy correspondence with the Company which proposed
to bring the railway to Barnard Castle, passing over his land
well to the south of Streatlam Castle.

'I do not consider the railway would be an advantage to
me personally,' Mr. Bowes wrote, 'but on the contrary,
passing where it does, and breaking in on our privacy, I
consider it a nuisance.' Sensibly, however, he saw that the
coming of the railway would be to the benefit of the town,
and he was prepared to allow it—on the one condition that
he should be provided with a private railway station, Broomielaw, to be reached by a private drive debouching from the
road opposite his park gates. The Railway Company agreed,

but Mr. Bowes was not entirely satisfied. 'Does the agreement,' he enquired of his solicitor, 'give me the power to stop a train to take up or put down a servant sent on business? I doubt it, but such was my intention.'

There was further correspondence regarding the station itself. 'It will be necessary,' he wrote, 'for me to have someone always living there, as at a lodge . . . they had better agree to build the cottage and they can let it to some respectable person, who will attend to the signalling, receiving the letter bags, etc.'

3

From 1841 onwards, life in Paris had begun to attract John Bowes more strongly than ever, and he spent more and more time there. He notified his solicitor and his Parliamentary agent that he did not intend to stand again for South Durham. He wished, he said, that he had taken his lawyer's advice and had kept out of politics, 'although my luck on the Turf will have about squared the matter'.

In 1847, having seen a young French actress, Mlle Delorme, playing at the Théâtre de Variétés in a piece called *Mademoiselle Grabutot*, he fell in love with her and, perhaps to further his suit, acquired a controlling financial interest in the theatre.

Mlle Delorme was the stage name of Mlle Joséphine Benoîte Coffin-Chevallier, la Contessa di Montalbo. Her grandfather, it was said, had been a clockmaker of Lyons. Her parents must have been rich, for they are supposed to have bought the title for their daughter from the miniature Republic of San Marino. As well as acting professionally, the Contessa was an amateur sculptor and a painter whose pictures were hung in the Paris *Salon*. Many of her canvasses can be seen in the Bowes Museum. It is customary to damn them with faint praise; yet she was no niggling amateur, content to throw off a few small pictures. She painted boldly and on a heroic scale—vast trees, gigantic houses, market baskets overflowing with fruit in prodigious quantities, and one of her landscapes, showing the Château de Louveciennes at the end of a woodland glade, is wholly delightful and completely satisfying.

In 1852 John Bowes became High Sheriff of County Durham. In 1854, at St. Marylebone Church, London, he married Joséphine Benoîte.

The wedding was a very quiet one, the only guests being Bowes' friend, Henry Morgan Vane, and Joséphine's maid. It seems possible that the marriage was, for a time, kept a secret, for no mention of his wife is made in any of Bowes' regular letters to his solicitor and to his agent until four years later when, on May 12th, 1858, he wrote to Mr. Dent asking him to purchase a 'quiet pony, to suit a very timid lady, say 12 or 13 hands, without any risk . . .' Four days later he writes, 'If you cannot get a pony, a donkey will do.' On July 18th he took Joséphine for the first time to Gibside to visit his mother. On July 26th he announces that they are going to Ardrossan for the sea-bathing; and, in preparation for Joséphine's first visit to Streatlam Castle, 'a sponging bath with turn-over sides to prevent the water running over when the maid empties it' was ordered.

In September Bowes, his wife, Lady Strathmore and Mr. Hutt arrived at Broomielaw Station by special train from Darlington. Madame Bowes, as she was always called in the North, had been unwell. The road from the station to the park gates had been specially smoothed and fish from Hartlepool and some good pale brandy had been obtained. There is no direct evidence, but it seems possible that an heir was eagerly expected. Such expectations, if they ever existed, were disappointed—which was an abiding sorrow to both of them.

After his marriage, Bowes had bought No. 7 Rue de Berlin, in Paris, and Joséphine seems to have entered wholeheartedly into her husband's passion for buying pictures. It may have been her influence which extended their joint purchases to tapestries, porcelain and china, furniture, and, in particular, to association pieces. In 1856, in his wife's name, Bowes had bought the Château de Louveciennes,

which Louis XV had built and furnished for Madame du
Barri. They divided their time, when they were in France,
between Louveciennes and the Rue de Berlin; but in 1862
the Château was sold and its furnishings and fittings shipped
over to Streatlam Castle.

It was between 1862 and 1864 that Mr. Bowes made his
largest and most important purchase of pictures. From the
widow of Francisco Xavier, Conde de Quinto, who had died
in 1860, he bought sixty-four pictures, among them the El
Greco 'St. Peter'; three Goyas; examples by Pereda, Antonio
Pere, Juan de Borgona, Antolinez, Carreno, Zubaran, F.
Camilo, Fray Juan Rizi, Valdes Leal and Antonio More; as
well as pictures representative of other European schools.

The Conde de Quinto was a Spanish politician and writer
who had been concerned with the preservation of works of
art. He had been Dean of the Central Commission for His-
torical and Artistic Monuments, and Director of the National
Museum of Paintings which had been instituted in 1838 to
house the works of art confiscated from the religious com-
munities of Madrid, Toledo, Avila and Segovia. Later, this
collection was incorporated in the Prado. In the course of
this transfer the most important pictures had been taken
over by the National Museum, and a large number of the
remainder had been sold. Quinto's collection would seem to
have been somehow amassed in the process.

4

In 1862 the idea occurred to Madame Bowes that their
joint collections should be assembled in a suitable building
and made available to the public. It is said that the notion
came to her while she and her husband were staying in
Calais, awaiting a calm crossing. She was a delicate woman
and suffered horribly from sea-sickness. John Bowes welcomed the idea; and, once the plan had taken root, their
purchases were more systematically directed towards the
end of assembling collections which would be representa-

JOHN BOWES

MRS. JOHN BOWES

tive of the various classes, styles, and periods of European art.

The site for the proposed Museum was to be in the neighbourhood of Calais. The idea, John Bowes always emphasized, had been his wife's. It was therefore fitting that the Museum should be on French soil and, at Calais, it would also look towards England. Jules Pellechet, member of a famous French dynasty of architects, prepared plans for an enormous building. Then everything was changed. Political events in France alarmed the Bowes'; France was considered, all of a sudden, far too unstable to serve as the permanent resting place for the collections; and in 1864 Mr. Bowes began negotiating for land on the outskirts of the small market town of Barnard Castle, only a few miles from Streatlam Castle.

Despite the fact that the Museum was to be built in County Durham and not in the Pas de Calais, Pellechet's original plans were to be retained; and these plans envisaged living quarters in the top storey of the Museum for Madame Bowes. She was many years younger than her husband; she expected to outlive him; and she wished to spend her widow-hood guarding and arranging the collections. It would appear that she was becoming reconciled—in the interests of her treasures—to English life.

In the early 1860's Streatlam Castle had at long last been completed—Mr. Bowes employing as his architect John Dobson, whose most notable achievement was the Central Railway Station at Newcastle upon Tyne. Dobson died in 1865, so Streatlam must have been one of the last of the many great houses of the North on which he worked. The balustraded terrace on which the house stood was completed; a new service wing was added to its east end; and water closets were installed. In 1864 Dobson built the fine orangery which is a near-replica of the orangery that George Bowes built at Gibside; and at the same time Mr. Bowes consulted a Mr. Glendenning regarding the planting of the park, the shrubberies, and the pinetum behind the house.

The Unhappy Countess

We have one glimpse of what life at Streatlam was like when Madame Bowes was in residence, for in September, 1861, Mrs. Davidson, Lady Anna Maria Jessup's only surviving daughter, brought her cousin Augustus Hare to pay a short visit to the Bowes'. An experienced stayer-away in country houses, Hare found this a strange experience, as he relates in *The Story of My Life*.

'*September 25th.*—I came with Cousin Susan to this curious place, to which my cousin, Mr. Bowes, has welcomed us so very cordially. The house is in a hollow—an enormous building of the last century, enclosing a mediaeval castle. I sleep in the ghost-room, looking most grim and weird from its black oak with red hangings, and containing a tall bed with a red canopy. "Here", the only existing Handbook says, "the unfortunate Mary Queen of Scots expired in captivity." I am afraid that the next Handbook will have to confess that she was beheaded at Fotheringay.

'The long galleries are full of family portraits—Hyltons, Blakistons, and Bowes'—one of whom, Miss Bowes of Streatlam, was Mrs. John Knox! More interesting to me is the great picture of Mary Eleanor, the unhappy Countess of Strathmore, walking in the grounds of St. Paul's Walden.

'*September 27th.*—This is the oddest house I ever was in! Everything is arranged for you, from the moment you get up till the moment you go to bed, and you are never allowed to deviate from the rules laid down: I even write this in time stolen from the half-hour for dressing. We are called at eight, and at ten march into breakfast with the same procession as at dinner, only at this meal "Madame Bowes" does not appear, for she is then reclining in a bath of coal-black acid, which "refreshes her system" but leaves her nails *black*. After breakfast we are all set down to employments appointed for the morning. At twelve Madame appears, having painted the under-lids of her jet-black eyes with belladonna. At two the bell rings for luncheon, and we are fetched if not punctual to an instant. At three we are all sent out driving (the coachman having exact orders where to take us) immense drives (twenty-four miles today) in an open barouche and pair. At seven we dine in great splendour and afterwards we sit in the oak drawing-room and talk about our ancestors!'

The project of establishing the Museum at Barnard Castle may have endeared Streatlam to Madame Bowes; and where Madame Bowes led, Mr. Bowes followed. In 1868—a further indication that their ties with Paris were weakening—the Théâtre de Variétés was sold; and on November 27th, 1869, Madame Bowes laid the Museum's foundation stone. It was a private ceremony attended only by Mr. and Mrs. Bowes; Mr. John Edward Watson, of Newcastle upon Tyne, associate architect for the building with M. Pellechet; and Mr. Joseph Kyle, of Barnard Castle, the master-builder. Madame Bowes' speech was brief. 'I lay the bottom stone,' she said, 'and you, Mr. Bowes, will lay the top stone.'

Building was begun in the following year.

Although the great iron entrance doors were to be cast in France, and French and Italian workmen were to be employed for the parquet floors and for the marble mosaics in the main hall, the building stone for the Museum came from two quarries on the Streatlam estate, while Mr. Watson's influence may have accounted for the choice of polished Aberdeen and Peterhead granite for the steps and columns of the principal staircase and of Craigleith granite for the landings.

The outbreak of the Franco-Prussian war, the siege of Paris, and the excesses of the Commune must have confirmed the Bowes' suspicions of French political stability. They themselves were at Streatlam during the siege, but the main parts of their collections were in Paris, and many of their most treasured possessions were removed for safety from the Rue de Berlin to the suburb of Vaugirard; and although the house in the Rue Blommet which had been rented to accommodate them was scarred by a bursting shell, its contents were not damaged. Bulletins were despatched by balloon by the Bowes' faithful servants and curators, the Chevriers.

The Unhappy Countess

A legal difficulty had arisen in connection with the founding of the Museum owing to the operation of the Mortmain Act (as it then stood); for it was discovered that Madame Bowes could not carry out her wish to build, endow and stock a museum dedicated to the public unless she conveyed the museum's site to trustees during her lifetime, and unless she lived for twelve months after the date of the deed of conveyance.

Madame Bowes had no wish to part with her Museum while she was alive. After her death she intended to bequeath everything for the public benefit, but she did not at all want to be interfered with by trustees while, as she confidently anticipated, she would be living as a widow in the upper storey of the building, queen of all she surveyed.

This difficulty was overcome by the introduction, in 1871, of a Parliamentary Bill—its sponsor was Bowes' step-father Sir William Hutt—to enable any person to bequeath, by will, subject to certain restrictions, land not exceeding twenty acres for any one public park, two acres for any one public museum, and one acre for any one schoolhouse. Under the title of The Public Parks, Schools and Museums Act (1871) the Bill became law; and Madame Bowes' will, dated July 12th, 1871, and a codicil dated July 19th, 1871, in fact established what she desired to be called The Joséphine and John Bowes Museum and Park.

The will devised to ten trustees (among them were her husband, Sir William Hutt, Henry Morgan Vane, A. W. Kinglake and Monsignor Witham) the land with the buildings on it and nineteen acres round it for the purposes of a public park. The codicil recited that she was possessed of a large number of pictures, books, works of art, and articles of furniture of great rarity and value; and that she was desirous that the same should not be dispersed. To this end the trustees were given instructions as to the placing of these collections in the Museum; and on the completion of this business—always provided that she had died in the meantime—they were to hand over the Museum, its contents, and the park, to a Committee of Management, the membership

196

of which was laid down. She left all her personal estate to the trustees as an endowment fund.

At the end of 1871 Mr. and Mrs. Bowes returned to Paris and began packing up certain of their treasures. In the following year more than a hundred packing cases were despatched to England and were stored at Streatlam Castle, as the Museum building was not yet ready to receive them.

In 1872 and 1873 the so-called 'coal famine' afforded colliery owners abnormally high prices for their coal; and they made very large but temporary profits. In these years John Bowes' income, from his colliery interests alone, exceeded £1,000 a day. So there was plenty of money available and the building of the Museum went gaily ahead.

Then Madame Bowes fell ill in Paris. On John Bowes' instructions, two blackbirds from Streatlam were sent to the Rue de Berlin, because he thought that their singing would please her. Meticulous instructions were given as to their care and feeding in transit. In February, 1874, Madame Bowes died, of a condition described as 'rheumatic bronchitis'. Her body was brought to England and was placed temporarily in the Gibside crypt, until such time as a Roman Catholic chapel in the park of the Museum should be built.

At the time of Madame Bowes' death the Museum was still a long way from being finished. The main walls were up, but progress had slowed down, probably on account of problems connected with the timbering of the roof, the importation of the French and Italian workmen, and the non-arrival of fittings from Paris.

Madame Bowes' trustees found themselves in what might have been a most difficult and embarrassing situation. They had been placed in possession of the land on which the Museum was being built, the land round it which was destined to be a public park, an unfinished building, and an exceedingly valuable collection of pictures, books, porcelain, furniture, and other works of art. But Madame Bowes had spent all her capital in buying the land at Barnard Castle, and she left, in fact, no personal estate whatever. There were, therefore, no funds available either for completing the Museum or for endowing it.

Mr. Bowes stepped into the breach and announced that he would complete the building as a memorial to his wife and would make himself responsible for the cost of its upkeep and maintenance. Further, he decided to donate to the Museum all his own valuable pictures and works of art, other than the Strathmore and Bowes possessions which had come to him from his father and which he scrupulously regarded as heirlooms which must follow the settled estates.

In 1875 the building of the Roman Catholic chapel in the park was begun. By 1880 the Museum itself, though still unfinished, had been roofed and was habitable, so the packing cases which had been stored at Streatlam were moved into it, and the first curator was appointed and took up residence.

It was at this juncture that a serious depression hit the coal trade, and Mr. Bowes, probably for the first time in his life, found himself short of ready money. As a result, between 1882 and 1885, little or no progress was made towards completing either the Museum or the chapel.

In the meantime John Bowes had married again, his second wife being a widow, la Comtesse de Courten. The marriage had turned out unhappy and he had secured a divorce. In the summer of 1885 he fell ill in Paris, apparently of the same dropsical disorder as had caused his father's death. In July, his doctors advised his return to England; and he died at Streatlam Castle on October 9th. The funeral, conducted in torrents of rain, involved a special train from Broomielaw station and burial in the crypt of Gibside chapel, where Madame Bowes' coffin, covered with immortelles, was still resting on its temporary trestles.

5

Mr. Bowes' obituary notices were numerous, long and appreciative. Perhaps the best of them appeared in the *Newcastle Daily Chronicle*, its author—was it Monsignor Witham? —surmounting the awkward hurdle of John Bowes' birth with a masterly simplicity. 'There is an old-fashioned sort of romance', he wrote, 'about the circumstances under which Miss Milner became Countess of Strathmore, but for obvious reasons it cannot be told here.'

Under the terms of his will, Mr. Bowes left the settled estates and a share in the residue of his personal estate to the Earl of Strathmore; and to the trustees of his wife's will trust he left legacies totalling £135,000, with a further contingent share of his personal estate. These legacies were intended to enable the trustees to complete the building of the Museum and the chapel and to provide them with a sufficient surplus which they could hand on to the Management Committee as an endowment fund to meet all maintenance costs once the Museum was finished and open to the public. Mr. Bowes also instructed his trustees and executors to select from his own effects such articles as they might think fit to be placed in the Museum, and to hand them over to his wife's trustees for that purpose.

On the face of it, the Bowes Museum trustees were in clover. All they had to do was to complete the building, transport the balance of the collections from Paris where they were still stored, arrange the contents, and hand over the Museum and the Park to the Committee of Management envisaged in Madame Bowes' codicil. In fact, their troubles had only just begun; and the survivors of those named by Madame Bowes—Monsignor Thomas Witham, A. W. Kinglake, Edward Young Western (a London solicitor), George Augustus Western, and Ralph John Dent, the Streatlam agent—must have rued the day they had ever heard of the project.

The trouble lay in the fact that, when he died, Mr. Bowes' financial position was very far from being a happy one. The depression in the coal trade had lasted for some years and John Bowes, Esq., and Partners had incurred heavy losses. Sir Mark Palmer owed Mr. Bowes' estate £120,892, and the value of this debt was in doubt. As a member of the partnership, Mr. Bowes, at his death, owed £159,000. Other debts amounted to £129,000. Furthermore, the payment of the legacies to the Bowes Museum trustees was contingent not only on his personal estate proving sufficient to pay off his debts in full, but also on the liquidation of other substantial legacies which ranked for payment before them.

The future of the Museum depended precariously on the salvaging of the fortunes of John Bowes, Esq., and Partners; and, most wisely, Bowes' executors declined to allow the Partnership to go into immediate liquidation, preferring to play for time. Mr. Bowes' estate was placed in Chancery, and in 1886 the Partnership was converted into a Limited Company.

But in the meantime the Museum trustees had on their hands the nearly but not quite completed building; the very valuable collections of which the items still stored in France had been seized by the French creditors and were being held in their interests; and precisely no income at all.

From Mr. Bowes' death until 1887 the trustees first dipped into their own pockets and then borrowed from the Bank on their personal responsibility. In 1887 they applied to the Charity Commissioners for leave to borrow money on a mortgage. In 1889 this permission was at last granted; but Bowes' executors still insisted on waiting until the affairs of the Company and the state of the coal trade would permit the sales of the assets which they possessed at what they considered an adequate figure.

The Museum trustees stuck grimly to their task in the face of considerable difficulties.

In the codicil to her will, Madame Bowes had addressed an exhortation to the people of Barnard Castle: 'And I request and adjure the inhabitants of Barnard Castle with a common accord to aid the Committee as far as possible in guarding the Museum, the contents of which it has taken so much of my time and trouble to collect and bring together, and their Park.'

The inhabitants of Barnard Castle wrongly interpreted this exhortation as meaning that the Museum and Park belonged to them; and they alternated between angry demands to the Museum trustees to hand over their responsibilities forthwith to the Committee of Management, and a very natural alarm that they would find themselves saddled with a Museum and Park and no revenue with which to maintain them.

In their own good time, and with the coal trade prospects brightening, the trustees finally decided to abdicate their responsibilities; and the Committee of Management—comprising the Lord Lieutenant of the County, the Member of Parliament, two nominees of the Lord Lieutenant, and 'so many other persons to be appointed by the trustees, and to be either rate-payers of the Parochial Chapelry of Barnard Castle, or to be resident within the said Chapelry, or within two miles thereof, as together with the trustees, etc., should make up eleven persons'—was duly constituted.

On June 10th, 1892, the Joséphine and John Bowes Museum and Park was formally opened by Sir Joseph Whitwell Pease, M.P. There was a procession, followed by a public luncheon. The procession was a notable one, and its components are perhaps worth recording.

The Band of the 3rd Battalion, the Durham Light Infantry; a Company of the 3rd Battalion, the Durham Light Infantry; Officials of the Court Leet; the Steward, and Manor Court; Justices of the Peace; Members and Officials of the Local Board of Health; the Fire Brigade, with engine drawn by horses; Members of the Board of Guardians; Members of the Mechanics' Institute; the Council of the Barnard Castle Agricultural Society; the Council of the Barnard Castle Horticultural Society; the Barnard Castle Lodge of Freemasons; the Manchester United Order of Oddfellows; the Ancient Order of Foresters; the Grand United Order of Oddfellows; the Sons of Temperance; the Weavers' Society; the Rail Servants' Society; the Members of the Building

The Unhappy Countess

Society; the Members of the Cricket Club; the Members of
the Teesdale Wanderers' Cricket Club; the Members of the
Excelsior Cricket Club; the Members of the Town Tennis
Club; the Members of the Harriers' Club; the Volunteer
Band and Company; the National Day and Church Sunday
Schools; the Wesleyan Methodists Day and Sunday Schools;
the Primitive Methodist Sunday School; the Roman Catholic
Day and Sunday School; the North Eastern County School;
and the General Public.

The approach from the railway station was decorated; and
the speakers, both at the opening of the Museum and at the
luncheon afterwards, said just exactly what one would have
expected them to say.

6

Teesdale, in the first half of the month of May, is one of
the most delectable parts of England. To the traveller from
the south, turning thankfully off the dull black racing-track
of the Great North road at Scotch Corner, its small stone
farm houses and cottages have a reassuring solidity and an
enviably simple elegance. The grass fields, with their neat
cut-and-laid hedges or stone walls, are prosperously and re-
freshingly green. The hand of the tree-feller has spared the
roadside sycamores. To the south, beyond browner fields
patched with gorse where the curlews call, is the line of the
moors. At the Greta there is now a new bridge alongside the
old one; but the woods of Rokeby and the great house itself,
glimpsed through its iron *claire-vue*, remain unspoilt. Turn
to the right down the by-road that skirts the park and passes
the Sphinx gates, and you will see ahead of you a wall of
trees on the further bank of the river, rounded tops rising
above rounded tops—pinkish brown, lime green, bright
green and golden yellow. Pay your sixpence to cross the toll
bridge above the brown Tees water flowing between flat
grey limestone rocks, scale the steep rise on the further side,
and soon, across the hedges to the north-west, you will see
something quite extraordinary—the great bulk of the Bowes

Museum, rising in splendid isolation and dominating the neat, unexciting countryside. Seen from this distance and from this angle it produces, momentarily, the impression of some gigantic and fabulous Oriental palace—the Potala, perhaps, as it is first glimpsed by the traveller as he approaches Lhasa.

A couple of miles further on, as you turn in through its gates and face the building squarely across a formal garden parterre terminated by a lofty terrace wall, you will see the Museum building for what it is—enormous, incongruous but immensely imposing. It has been variously described and assessed by startled visitors viewing it for the first time. Dr. Pevsner has observed that it looks exactly like the Town Hall of a major provincial city in France. Sir Albert Richardson, P.R.A., gained the impression of a château that had been transported by a magician from France, and it struck him as incredible that such a building should fit in so well with the Northern landscape. Mr. Humphry House regarded it as a foreign aristocrat, transplanted with a good deal of sang-froid and at least a touch of vulgarity.

Whether it is conceded or denied that it is an astonishing building to find on the outskirts of a small grey market town in County Durham, most people will agree that it houses the most catholic and endearing of museums; and its contents have been lovingly and skilfully weeded and arranged by its present curator, Mr. Thomas Wake.

The first impression, on entering its enormous hall, is one of cold polished grandeur, which the great pink granite staircase does nothing to dispel. The silent, antique hydraulic lift, controlled by a rope and tucked away in the farthest corner of the building, is a more appropriate method of reaching the two main exhibition floors, each with twenty-two inter-connecting rooms. And here the initial chill is at once dispelled, because each room has been arranged *as a room*—whether it is an eighteenth-century gentleman's library, a mediaeval chapel, Madame du Barri's bedroom, or a series of galleries hung with the kind of pictures that you might just conceivably find in some great country house.

The Unhappy Countess

There are glazed museum cases, it is true, but their ugly black-painted woodwork has been stripped and delicately marbled, so that they have miraculously become things of beauty in themselves.

The most important of the pictures, El Greco's 'St. Peter', the Goyas, the Boucher landscape, Reynolds' portrait of Mrs. Thrale, David's 'Napoleon I', the Sasseta, Tiepolo and other Italian pictures, and the canvasses by Champaigne, Fragonard, Corot, Fantin-Latour and Boudin are displayed in the galleries, arranged in periods and set off by tapestries, by panelling, and by such delectable surprises as an enormous and perfectly lovely carpet worked in cross-stitch by the grand-daughter of Barbara Villiers, Duchess of Cleveland. But there are also important pictures hanging on the walls of all the other rooms, such as the fifteenth-century Dutch Triptych by the Master of the Virgo inter Virgines. John Davidson's library of eighteenth-century books from Ridley Hall—left to John Bowes by Augustus Hare's 'Cousin Susan' —is concentrated in one room, but in many of the other rooms there are also books in fine bindings, just as there would be in the rooms of a well-furnished country house. English porcelain; the great collections from the Vincennes and Sèvres manufactories; the Meissen and other European porcelain and pottery; and the Oriental collections are concentrated in individual rooms, but again specimens spill over into other apartments as they would in the house of a private collector; and there is a fascinating dining-table set out with an array of tureens in the shapes of a boar's head, a hare, hen-and-chickens and cabbages, and with fruit, nuts, sliced eggs, asparagus and artichokes modelled in earthenware and porcelain. In a suite of rooms in the French taste, one bedroom contains the furnishings from Madame du Barri's Château de Louveciennes, and another pieces from No. 7 Rue de Berlin. In the 'children's room' there is an entrancing life-sized working model in silver of a fish-swallowing swan, made by an Englishman, Weekes, in 1790, bought at the 1867 Paris Exhibition by Napoleon III for the Prince Imperial, and subsequently purchased by Mr. Bowes; and an immense picture of a Durham Shorthorn by John Glover. You pay your money and you take your choice.

Nowadays, many English country houses are open once more to the public, and the family possessions are displayed to their best advantage. The Bowes Museum affords just such an opportunity for enjoyment on a scale unprecedented in any individual house. Not everything in the varied collections is of the first water; but the best may be said to gain, rather than to lose, by that.

Most of the pictures, furniture, tapestries, silver, ivories and porcelain—to say nothing of the geological specimens and the contents of the rooms displaying typical features of nineteenth-century Teesdale—were collected by the Bowes'. But certain exhibits have been lent by the National Collections, others have come as gifts, others (including the Ormonde plate) are on loan from private Collections. Nor is the collection a static, finished, petrified affair. Acquisitions have not been confined to making the collections of English works of art comparable to those of other European countries—although this has been the main aim in recent years. Quite lately Mr. Wake, with financial help from the National Arts Collections Fund and from other sources, succeeded in buying a Louis XV dressing table in tulip wood and rosewood, with ormolu mounts. It is stamped '*Garde Meuble de la Reine: M.A.*' and came from the Petit Trianon. It was, Mr. Wake explains, exactly the kind of association piece—and the collection is rich in association pieces—that Mr. and Madame Bowes could never have resisted. And such a purchase, surely, shows that the collecting spirit of the Bowes' lives on.

7

But the true heart of the museum is to be found in the Bowes room. The pictures on its walls were painted by Joséphine, the furniture is from the drawing-room of No. 7 Rue de Berlin, John Bowes' racing cups and other personal mementoes are there, and so are the intimate souvenirs of the nineteenth-century Kings of France which the Bowes' collected so assiduously and treasured so greatly. And here, on either side of a white porcelain stove, hang the portraits of John Bowes and of his wife—Joséphine, small, dark-haired, with snapping black eyes and a determined, rat-trap mouth; John with his heavy, long, good-natured, whiskered face, whimsical but solid. It is related that when his friend Monsignor Thomas Witham first saw this portrait he observed, 'Ah, yes. That's my old friend Bowes, sure enough, dressed like his own gamekeeper and surrounded with more game than he ever shot in his life.'

Were they happy, these two apparently ill-assorted human beings?

Of Joséphine's origins we know so little. There was the grandfather who was a Lyons clockmaker; the ambitious parents who turned their daughter into a Contessa. She herself must have had a powerful urge for self-expression. One imagines her clever, determined, autocratic, acquisitive —with a vitality which overstrained a weak constitution but which must have appealed strongly to her melancholy-inclined husband. An alien figure, with her bella-donna'd eye-lids and her blackened finger-nails, in the settings of Streatlam Castle and Gibside; much more at home among her collections than in the company of the County Durham and Yorkshire neighbours. She had no children, and that was an abiding sorrow. There are an unusual number of sculptured children's figures in the Museum, some of them terribly banal. She collected them greedily.

John Bowes' background has been described in these pages —the slur of illegitimacy; the material wealth which cannot fail to influence a man's character; the shrewd, quiet, commonsense dignity of his mother keeping within bounds the kindly, undisciplined passions of his father; the innate good taste and love of beautiful things which, combined with a hard-headed business sense, came to him from his great-grandfather, George Bowes, by way of his extraordinary, ill-balanced, clever, unfortunate grandmother.

It is appropriate that these two people—misfits they might

perhaps have been called—who shared a common interest in the theatre and in the arts should have left behind them so strange, so moving and, outwardly, so theatrical and incongruous a memorial.

8

There are a few loose ends of the story to gather up.

It was in 1905 that the Committee of Management at last got its legacy from John Bowes' personal estate, receiving £125,000 out of the £135,000 named in his will. And on this endowment the Museum and Park existed quite happily until the devaluation of the pound rendered its annual income disastrously insufficient. The Durham County Council has accepted a proposal that it should assume the trusteeship of the Museum and has undertaken to make good the annual excess of expenditure over income.

The Roman Catholic chapel in the Bowes Park, which was unfinished at John Bowes' death although he had spent some £8,000 on its building, was removed from its original site by the Museum's trustees in 1927 and rebuilt just outside the Park wall—an action which John Bowes would surely have found difficult to forgive. In 1929 his coffin, and that of Madame Bowes, were removed from the crypt at Gibside and interred in a vault outside the chapel. His great-grandfather, George Bowes, that man of taste, would not wholeheartedly have approved of the lettering on the granite slab that marks their grave.

Although the park of Streatlam Castle is well maintained, the house which William Blakiston Bowes built, and in which Lady Strathmore was imprisoned, has been pulled down. It served as a battle-school in the last war, and one wonders if any of the infantrymen in training saw the ghosts of pitmen shouting round their bonfires or the figure of the unhappy Countess riding pillion behind Chapman on her way to Gowland's cottage.

The Unhappy Countess

The Forestry Commission has taken over the Gibside policies, and has covenanted to preserve the surviving features of George Bowes' great landscape layout. The chapel has always been well kept up—it was endowed by the 10th Earl—and a service is held in it each Sunday. A wreath of immortelles from Madame Bowes' coffin still lies in one of the niches in its crypt.

Index

The Unhappy Countess

Index